LET HER PLAY

MRS. D,

WHO WOULD HAVE THOUGHT WE'D BE HERE?
A BOOK? YOU KNOW THIS WHOLE WRITING
THING STARTED WITH YOU, RIGHT? I RECENTLY
FOUND THE OLD 'CHRONICLES OF JEFF & AARON'
AND WAS IN TEARS - JOYFUL AND NOSTALGIC.
YOU'VE BEEN SUCH AN AMAZING INFLUENCE
IN MY LIFE & MANY OTHERS. AND
I COULDN'T BE MORE GRATEFUL. THIS
BOOK IS YOUR WIN AS MUCH AS
MINE. WITH LOTS OF LOVE.

[signature]

Commentary from those influenced by this book's philosophies

From former players:

"You always made it fun and really helped me gain confidence again, even when I would come down on myself, you were there to bring me back up." – **Mallory**

"One of my favorite aspects of the way you coached was that even though you were focused on developing soccer, you also formed personal connections with the players. I felt like I could trust you with much more than just soccer." – **Casey**

"You were a very motivational coach. You were one of the first coaches to tell us to visualize in our heads what we wanted to do. You were the first to tie in the injury prevention, outside training, and healthy eating into soccer. Most other coaches just told you to eat well, but you made sure we knew what that really meant. Another thing is how you still care even after I've left the team. You stuck with me through years of my recovery and it's helped to have so much support. You become more than just a coach to your players. You're more like a friend or older brother." – **Emily**

"There are two things that I appreciated the most. One, you never made us do anything which you weren't prepared to do yourself. I've had coaches who sat back, didn't work hard, and berated their athletes for mistakes. You never did that. You were often on the line with us, sprinting as hard as you could, encouraging us while easily running us into the ground. It wasn't just physical work that you did, though. I've never had a coach that planned practices as well as you did. We often had practices during which we would focus on one particular thing, and we would have interesting,

complicated, and difficult drills to help us with that. Sometimes coaches fall into a routine, but you never did. You worked hard. It was always a mentality of 'I'll do my work, and you'll do yours. Maybe we'll mess up, and then we'll work to fix that.'

"Two, you cared about us as people. Some coaches look at their players as that and only that: players. They're not individual people; they only exist for the coach on the playing field. Once you go home, once you leave the pitch, you cease to exist beyond a statistic or a number. You always respected us as players and also as human beings. You wanted us to grow as players and also as human beings. You were dedicated to us—to our growth, to our health, to our wellbeing. Right off the heels of playing on [my old] team, when I was in a terrible spot as an athlete in terms of my self-confidence, your team was right where I needed to be." – **Aidan**

"I think what I most appreciated about your coaching was that you taught us not only how to be better players but how to be better people. In my experience coaches have often neglected to see how intertwined success is on the field with character off the field. How are you supposed to build a team if everyone is in it for themselves? Playing for you taught me not only how to play defense on the field but how to collaborate and be a leader in the classroom and beyond." – **Anna**

From Parents of Players:

"To coach a young girl in soccer is to take the role of father, brother, uncle, mentor, and friend and provide these young ladies with encouragement, accountability, care, and love so that they can feel free to explore, make mistakes, and grow. Aaron, you did this beautifully. Thank you! Oh yeah, and taught them something about soccer, the beautiful game!" – **Brad**

"We believe you were the best soccer coach that our daughter has had!" – **Mary**

"Aaron made a connection with my daughter to understand her soccer goals and work to achieve those goals. However, more importantly, he taught her life lessons through soccer that she will use the rest of her life." – **Joe**

"Coach Aaron is more than coach. He is a mentor and a role model. He is one of those coaches that make an impact and that you wiii never forget! I am so proud of all your successes. You are a true influence on the kids and parents as well." – **Kelly**

I thought practices were running over and I thought it was on you, only to discover it was Claire enjoying connecting with you and players in a fun and nurturing environment. She has always had a voice, and you allowed her to express herself on and off the field. – **Christine**

Aaron's approach to coaching has greatly impacted my daughter's self-esteem and confidence, far beyond the sports field – **LWM**

LET HER PLAY

AARON VELKY

Let Her Play

Printed in the United States of America
ISBN 978-1-946425546

Book Design by CSinclaire Write-Design

To all the people who helped me
be of strong character
so that I could help others develop
strong character,
thank you.

Contents

PREFACE

There's been such a struggle internally writing this book. As time went on, fear was more and more crippling, and I felt like I didn't have a clean, simple way to illustrate what I hope to offer to you in this writing.

Then it happened.

Two players of mine both shared a message in a single week that demonstrates what this book represents as aspiring impact.

It made it clear. I believe there are two things players want from their parents:

- Safety in how they can share, express, and be themselves
- Space to make their own mistakes, learn, and own their destiny

The goal of *Let Her Play* is to turn this:

Hi Coach!

I remember in the beginning of the year at the team meeting you said that us players should tell you when soccer isn't that enjoyable. Honestly, I think it's becoming less fun for me. I'm letting my personal life get in the way, which is stressful.

I feel uncomfortable exposing my personal life. But if you don't mind me telling you, I just don't have a great family life.

I don't receive much support because in fact . . . I get told that I'm unworthy of love constantly from my parents, seriously. So I'm running solo and I'm my own supporter. Honestly, soccer was an escape from my problems, now it seems like a chore in a way. I don't know what I'm trying to get out of this email but I think I just need help. Since you're my coach, I feel that I should reach out to you.

I feel super guilty that I always go to you at the end of practices/games but I just want this sport to be fun again. I know this email may be hard to respond to but any advice would be nice to hear. Thanks for your time.

Into this:

When I started playing club soccer in sixth grade, I was a somewhat shy, goofy middle schooler with average athletic talent. I ran a 10 minute mile and was not the best player on my team by a sizable margin. At one particularly bad practice, my first coach told me that I'd never be good. And then I met Aaron Velky.

Aaron pushed us hard. We ran more sprints and did more lunges than almost any team in the club. But we weren't alone; Aaron was at our side for every run we ran and every flight of stairs we climbed, encouraging us when we wanted to quit and reminding us why our burning muscles were worth it. That extra fitness only served to make us better, faster, and hungrier for more. By eighth grade, my mile time had dropped to a 6:30 pace. Two years after that, I made a team at the time ranked third in the state.

Many coaches determine success solely by win-loss records and rankings. Aaron wasn't like that. All he ever asked for was our maximum effort and dedication, and if we gave him 110%, he didn't care what the score was.

Aaron taught us that soccer is much more than what happens on the field. He taught us to lead with integrity. He helped to make me the hard-working, self-assured person I am today. He showed me that more than anything else, success is won by fierce grit and determination. I can only hope that he continues to pass on his wisdom to dozens more aspiring girls like me in the years ahead.

I've realized my job as a coach isn't to drive the team

to glory, to win championships, or to create millionaire athletes.

My job is to be what my players need me to be, for them, for their futures, so that they may be their best selves.

I've written this guide to all I've learned both from failure to be what my players need in search of my own glory as well as from the moments of the most significant connection that have allowed players to become the versions of themselves they didn't even realize were possible.

Thanks for picking up this book. I hope you're as committed to your daughter as I am committed to supporting you in the process of supporting her.

INTRODUCTION

I've had to consistently revisit a powerful why to get over the fear associated with publishing this book.

It's a simple purpose: to provide parents of young female athletes the most important lesson I've learned in nearly a decade of my coaching perspective.

Delivery, though, requires tact.

To open up your eyes to some of the things happening, I will shock you. I will challenge your traditional practices on the sidelines and at home. I will challenge your objectives and intentions. And while it may be uncomfortable, the lesson will blossom beautifully.

Seven years of coaching young women has taught me a lot.

Mostly that we're missing the point.

I remember some of my most important moments as a coach.

One day, while my phone buzzed fielding nasty emails and aggressive texts about my inattentiveness at practice, I had to silence my notifications. They were coming in too fast. I wondered if I should be honest. I was inattentive, no doubt.

I left the team self-managing the warmup while I took a walk with a player who was crying. It took me a long time to return. There was no denying it.

Two weeks later she was admitted on suicide watch. There was a letter. A plan.

My heart crumbled getting that message from her family.

What could I have done better?

I should have done more!

I failed.

I felt so crippled. So weak. So ashamed.

Not only had I not done enough, but I was walking with her and felt my phone going off and started to feel anxious. My mind was worried about how quickly we would get back. I knew people were watching. So I wasn't present. In her moment of need, I wasn't present. Worried about parent backlash, I lost a moment to maybe change a life.

Which would you prioritize—a young girl who needed emotional support from someone she could trust or prepping for another soccer game that we would all forget?

Another day I got a call from a mom as I drove to training. No details, just a request to talk before we started. When I arrived, she and her daughter were hugging each other and in tears, waiting for me.

My heart sank. I knew something was not just wrong but broken.

Her husband didn't wake up the night before, he was blue. Dead in his sleep. Naturally, she and her daughter were devastated, baffled, lost, hurt, and raw.

She asked me to tell the team so that the girls could offer support.

I nearly threw up.

How do I do this?

Why me?

Why today?

Through tears, tears I hadn't shed for myself in

years, I shared that we'd lost a part of the team. Not a player, but that a family member passed in the night. There wasn't a time to prepare.

Here I was, trying to force strength through my words, trying to see me through their eyes, trying to be a good man for them to lean on.

I was the best I could be, and I saw it all as if my soul had walked out of my body and watched as we all shared one big embrace.

That girl and I went on a walk nearly every day for a month.

Some of that team, through the challenges, have become best friends and taken away lessons from major life happenings. A token of prioritizing the right things.

So as I write this and recall these stories, I'm both heartful and scared. Those moments taught me so much as a coach.

Still to this day I get letters and emails and texts from some of my players. They don't tell me their soccer success stories. They tell me how important it was to be given space to be themselves, to be heard, to be appreciated, respected, and trusted. Instead of reprimanding, they were afforded opportunities and reflections.

Those girls taught me so much.

Now it's my turn to teach you.

While we are all screaming from the sidelines, reprimanding referees, and judging our coach's decision, we're missing the opportunities to impart real learning, wisdom, and serenity to these young women.

I deeply want your daughter to be successful at her sport. I hope she loves it as much as I love soccer. I hope she loves basketball or track or volleyball or whatever her sport. I hope one day she can give back to the game that has given to her.

I hope she makes you proud.

But I hope your definition of "success" in this pursuit of sporting glory is softened by reading this.

It's with grace that I write and share this.

Thanks for choosing to step into grace.

LET HER PLAY

PROLOGUE

I'm sitting in my basement watching the USA play China in the 2015 Women's World Cup. I've coached for years at this point, but watching Kelly O'Hara walk off the pitch with a bloody nose was awful, alarming, and, strangely, fortuitous for me personally. There wasn't any emotion on her face. She wasn't crying. She wasn't fearful. She wasn't angry. I saw her lips mouth the words, "It's not broken. I'm OK." to her coach. If there were ever a moment, as a coach, that personified so vividly the things I want to illuminate, it was this one.

I'm not a prolific coach. You won't see me on TV or with a national team. I'm just a guy who has worked with hundreds of young women through soccer and my other businesses. In my role, in so many varied ways, I am responsible for supporting young women as they grow into accomplished athletes and successful adults. Those two aren't always the same.

What kind of role model was I going to be? How was I

going to give them what they needed to be their most successful? How could I contribute to building strong women? How might I uplift them? How can I help build and shape them?

I realized over the years that much of that has to do with who is around them. If I'm only around them five hours a week, what about the other 163 hours? How might I make sure they get quality influence at home?

I've put together a recipe to develop the skills, mind-set, and appetite needed to be successful as an athlete. The last few years I've offered exclusive one-on-one training to several athletes, and while we spend hours developing goals, refining their mindset, and opening up their capacity to learn, none of this involves as much physical training as you'd think.

Nurturing the whole person, of which the athlete is only a part, is a pathway I never would have estimated to have the kind of impact it does. It speaks as the example of what happens when the influences that are around us most often, with significant time investment, shape us most.

With a few families, I've been able to offer something incredibly special. It took a lot of investment from all of us—parents, the student (athlete), and from me. When we delved deeply into subjects like process, the growth mindset, failure, creativity, stress management, and more, several amazing things happened. Grades went up, and the management of schoolwork, family, and sports became more efficient with more success.

Even the conversations at home deepened. Armed with topics for each month, exercises, and drills, the athletes have all blossomed—on and off the field.

Ahead you'll find my most deeply meaningful strategies, cultivated over years of triumphs and heartaches. I hope to challenge you to think differently about your perspective as a parent of a young athlete. This book is about showcasing the constructs of human relationships that allow for the most fluid and natural talent expansion. In addition, we'll try to identify some of the nefarious enemies of rapid growth. First, a few assumptions so that you understand the context of this book:

1. *You are a parent or coach who's interested in the betterment of your daughter and can set aside your own wants and needs to place hers first.*

2. *If you read an example of a parent displaying less-than-exemplary behavior, you can read it and consider what similarities it may draw to your own behaviors without judging yourself but with lots of love in the hope of deepening and improving the behavior in the interest of your daughter.*

3. *The purpose of picking up a book like this is to better your athlete and better the relationship you have with her, and you're willing to do the difficult things to provide what she needs to thrive, even if the difficult thing is doing less or nothing.*

Sometimes the truth can be hard to hear. Sometimes we may choose to avoid it, refusing to accept that a particular behavior is one we've displayed ourselves. It will take brutally honest introspection to fully develop a changed perspective that comes from deep, meaningful work. But while offering you that moment, I realize that I have to be brave.

I have to stand up for the girls that I've coached—some of whom are living under rules, expectations, and standards that could never create success. Whether it be in sports, in the classroom, or in their careers, I hope that the stories and perspectives shared here provide ideas and strategies for you to embrace at home, in the car, and on the sidelines.

You see, Kelly O'Hara was just one example of a strong athlete on the field during that world cup game. Nearly all of these athletes had mastered themselves. They had dedicated years to perfecting their craft and years to mastering their mindset. This same mastery is needed in business people, in teachers, in CEOs, and in our young women who aren't going to be top athletes too.

Failure, determination, resilience, toughness, focus, and passion all combined to create a woman I couldn't help but respect. The bloody nose was just an example of a barrier she chose to overcome. One of many.

But overcoming barriers must become a habit if we are to achieve anything meaningful in our life, requiring us to revisit our relationship with barriers, struggle, conflict, challenge, and defeat.

Those things don't always come naturally, but with good coaches, parents, and leaders around our young women, I do believe they can become examples of those descriptions too. No matter where their future takes them, we should let the athletic experience develop key character components.

When we choose to allow our players to have moments that test them, without our interjection, we get to see just how resilient they are. Proudly, we can watch them become their best selves.

This book is a recipe for how we do that. Because these moments that test our players are meant to be difficult, and if we want to develop strong women on or off the field, we must be able to separate ourselves from the natural instincts we get to protect them and shield them.

This is about anti-entitlement in its raw form (which I recognize is a bit of a buzzword), but against it in the truest form of love and respect I can muster from my bones.

Most often, we are missing the chances to do that in our need to feel validated, to feel like our expectations have been met, and to feel like our expenses of time and money are worth it. But together we'll walk through the processes needed for young women to become the athletes they could be.

I've had to fill the shoes of older brother, dad, friend, confidant, counselor, and therapist in so many of my days coaching. What follows is a system of being and behavior that have allowed my players to thrive—not as players, as people.

I believe that when we support the whole person, the athlete thrives. This book is the process by which I choose to lead. It isn't perfect, neither is my writing. I do attest that many parents and players feel strongly that these methods have deeply impacted their lives and future, and we as leaders of these women should bear in mind the endgame of this sporting experience.

If we want success, we must realize it's out of our control for the most part.

The hard part is consciously, intentionally letting go. She wins when we can consciously and intentionally let go.

We have to *Let Her Play.*

CHAPTER 1

Evaluation: Tryouts, Team Placement, and Disappointment

"Whoever is careless with the truth in small matters cannot be trusted with important matters."

Albert Einstein

Evaluation as a Requirement of Youth Development

Evaluation is a part of adult life.

Being evaluated is not the outcome; it's the process. And it's a process that I've come to love. Any athlete should.

As adults, we go through it all the time. We learn to

accept it, and those who find massive success learn to master it. Those who don't master it end up suffering from it.

In my years of coaching soccer, it's been amazing to see what kids can handle and to observe how they handle it. When equipped with the right tools, they are incredibly adept—more adept than we adults ever credit them for being—at taking tough news and using it as motivation. Often, they deal with criticism and failure better than adults do, but we adults tend to poison their thoughts by implanting our own insecurities.

Have you ever had a friend tell you a dream, and your insecurities screamed, "It's unsafe to quit your job," or "No chance that works out! Don't risk it!"? I once told a young player that she wasn't fast or strong enough to play with us yet, but if she worked really hard, she could participate in tryouts again in a few months.

Mom was upset, but I was honest and gentle in my delivery, and I gave her the chance to try again. She didn't listen to the insecurities, and the next year, she became my starting forward, scoring half the team's goals that season. She told me that being cut was the wake-up call she needed to start working hard. Without that, she would have kept straddling between soccer and other interests. That setback became the catalyst for her success.

Another player, when faced with relegation to my team in her eighth grade year, decided that she did not want to invest her time in soccer, that she was more interested in lacrosse, and she went on to play varsity lacrosse at a very reputable high school lacrosse program.

My experiences have shown me that evaluation and feedback are critical to success in any field. That's why this chapter is all about how we as caregivers can be more comfortable with both. Often we are the ones stewing over these processes and creating a dark stormy cloud because of them.

When left to their own devices, young women are incredibly strong and more emotionally resilient than we expect them to be. In both of the above cases, the perceived failure meant a sea change that culminated in a better path. Young women can handle more than we adults let them. Please let that sink in. More than we ***let*** them.

We want to protect them, but instead we shelter them and weaken their resolve. Allowing them to have this tempering experience is the most loving thing we can do most times, even if it may be hard to watch.

Still, walking the tight rope between letting them grow strong independently and following the impulse to protect and shelter is exceptionally difficult—I'm not a parent, and even I get that.

But the most amazing things happen with young athletes when they can develop confidence of their own. Not only do they produce more on whatever field or court they occupy but they will take more risks and put in more heart. Still, supporting their build-out of confidence is the tough part, and evaluation is often perceived as the most diabolical part of it, despite it being so recurrent in the growth of a child. However, without evaluation and the challenges it offers, we are not preparing our future women leaders to withstand pressure, challenge, and results-oriented living. We are sheltering them from inevitable storms, and the more we protect them, the more damaging future storms are.

Whether it be the team they join, the game they lost, the round of tryouts they didn't make, or the skill they are struggling to develop, the most important fundamental action we can take as adults supporting young daughters is to help them navigate the process of deciding what should occur next.

In the stories of both players I mentioned earlier, we see a common thread: **Those players' parents supported evaluation and the challenges that come with and from it rather than redirecting hardship and sheltering the girls from painful emotional experiences. The girls learned to deal with their losses in a healthy way and were allowed to promote their own growth.**

I am evaluated a dozen times a day in my life. I'm sure you face that too. When I am evaluated, I learn how I should improve, and if I indeed meet the challenge, I recognize that many more instances of evaluation will follow every success.

I'm evaluated as a coach: Poor performances,

inappropriate comments, or bad behavior could leave me jobless. I'm evaluated as an artist: If my work is not original or fails to satisfy my client, I will not be paid, nor should I be. I was evaluated at my corporate job as well. Yearly reviews were opportunities to discuss how well I was doing and whether or not I was meeting expectations. I'm evaluated as an entrepreneur. Not everyone I pitch to invests, not every potential client writes a check, not every institution is interested in teaching young adults about money and careers.

Evaluation is unavoidable. The faster we accept this, the faster evaluation can be utilized as a tool for growth.

My point here is a two-part idea:

One: Life is a continuous battle, and as you grow older, evaluation isn't just a tool for "team placement"—it's the single most important catalyst for self-awareness.

Two: Those who seek opportunities to be challenged and evaluated, and thus are less averse to failure, shall rise more quickly than those who actively avoid those opportunities.

Sports teaches the most astonishing things and produces the most resilient people, but that cannot happen unless the proper environment is created around the young athlete. Evaluation itself is a consistent evolutionary element. Survival of the fittest is a naturally occurring environmental circumstance, and because the process is one of natural evaluation, we see the emergence of dominant traits. In similar fashion, there are elements to being evaluated that can help young adults thrive.

The Results of Evaluation

Evaluation carries with it several important results. Most successful people, in any field, will attest that they've experienced these. The truly great admit that they are grateful for all of them.

In an age where we reward mediocrity with participation trophies and other vehicles that reinforce a generalized nonchalance, evaluation often seems cold. But as we explore the results of evaluation, I want you to challenge your concept of it so that we can usher in some new healthy ideas.

Evaluation works primarily around four circumstances:

1. *Suffering Defeat*
2. *Managing Frustration and Disappointment*
3. *Overcoming Obstacles*
4. *Achieving Success*

Each of these contributes to the whole person of the athlete; however, each becomes much more intimidating as you climb in age.

What would your relationship with your daughter look like if you held these four as important parts of the process, rather than condemning comments that she should be sheltered from?

"No legacy is so rich as honesty."
William Shakespeare

Evaluation is about honesty. It's about letting someone feel what truth is.

I think we can all agree honesty is important.

Yet on a regular basis, the honesty of evaluation is not respected.

Great soccer players—and most great athletes—hate losing. It's built into the lust for winning, but all great athletes understand that losses and losing are part of the experience no matter how devastating they might be. More importantly, they've learned from losses and know how to benefit from that learning. They may not call it "data," but analyzing what their minds and bodies do when they lose (both consciously and subconsciously) is creating knowledge. They learn exactly how to improve their skill, but more substantially, they learn how to manage the loss of confidence.

A useful and instant peek into the mindset of young athletes comes from pulling them aside in a losing match and asking them an open-ended question. Too often we give youth the easy-out that comes with a yes-or-no inquiry. As you know, water will always find the path of least resistance. Often so do easy answers! Instead, I ask for their thoughts. I might ask them, "What do you think we should adjust?"

As players learn that it's expected that they be cognizant of what is causing defeat and expected that they make adjustments and recover, they begin to evolve the mindset of an observer (a product of environment) into the mindset of a manipulator (an interactive component of environment). Though that change does not directly correlate with how they will deal with more emotional aspects of sports participation, it does become an integral part of understanding failures. This evolution also corresponds directly to that which is needed to become incredible at *anything*. Those who can think, read, and play intelligently can advance, and that requires us to consider how valuable feedback can be and how iteration, then, is the pinnacle of possibility.

This happens most often after losses. While it is important to analyze wins, it's certainly more natural to try to understand why we did not succeed. If we deny our young adults the chance to do that, we are curbing their coping mechanism and their ability to think their way out of challenges.

Young adults often confuse winning with the most important part of the game, and while I instill in my players that winning is important, it is inauthentic to place our youth only in situations where they are guaranteed wins. Not only does that undermine valuable lessons gained from suffering defeat but it also dilutes the achievement behaviors that are so vital to nurturing successful women. My rule of thumb for young teams: A team that wins every game is playing in the wrong league, just as a team that loses every game is as well. A healthy youth team should go 50-50.

Engineering repeated wins creates a cavity in development.

Instead of players feeling confident consistently through ups and downs, we are actually preparing them for a confidence cliff dive. An evaluation opportunity that goes south can quickly erode their entire athletic-emotional balance. Suddenly, the series of wins seems instead like a series of flukes, and the trust in themselves and the team is hard to recover because they haven't actually developed the skill of managing frustrations and overcoming obstacles.

As children grow into puberty and young adulthood, management of frustration becomes a more consequential understanding. Without a viable outlet, the situational extremes become more and more identifiable for young adults as the influences of social media can twist a docile mind into one more cognizant of behaviors that are violent. Evaluation provides a simple and effective way to give young adults experience dealing with frustration and aggression. Without a successful example and a healthy opportunity to attempt to mimic that example, young adults simply wonder what they should do with such a large rush of energy and unfamiliar adrenaline.

Thankfully, most athletes find opportunities to release the frustration they might feel in games or practices. It is a coach's responsibility to foster an environment that both creates and allows for that. A good coach will successfully create happenstances that place young players in positions to be frustrated and overwhelmed.

That coupling is the simplest to create and is the most crucial for development. And the best coaches will coach not only the skills players need to win but also the habits players need to deal with loss.

Because of the constant need to be better, stronger, and smarter than other players on the pitch, wise coaches link hard work and dedication to success. When a young athlete can demonstrate and internalize a direct correlation between hard work and dedication and overcoming some real or created obstacle, it sends a very powerful signal across learning channels in the brain. Not only does the brain latch on to that work-reward system but also it creates a faster transmission line for that same signal. In short, the more you learn to conquer obstacles, the more you conquer obstacles. If you want to learn more about this, check out Daniel Coyle's *The Talent Code*.

But what about at home? What if there isn't a coach around?

There is an important element of grace that can be invited into the home on the subject of evaluation. With every evaluation that your daughter goes through, it may feel like you too are being evaluated.

You may feel as if you failed if she gets a poor grade or if people are calling her names. You may feel as if you've done a bad job raising her if she's not the top player on a team, and your ego may bark at you if she's not playing every single minute of the game.

But I would invite you to recall this: Her life and her situations are there as invitations to grow. They are not there to judge you, your parenting, or your genetics.

Her experiences and yours are separate.

Her evaluations, whether positive or negative, will be a great opportunity for you to support her and help her understand how the outcome is an unfolding process that begins with failure before it can end in success.

An introverted yet inquisitive 11-year-old girl who was having trouble in math asked for her father's help. As he proclaimed with humility that he could not help with the specific set of math questions, she consoled him with a soft, "Don't worry, Daddy, I wasn't very good at left-footed passing, and I worked at it, and now I'm good. I'll just keep working on this and eventually, I'll be good at it."

Evaluation Is Worthless If It Doesn't Involve Struggle and Even Failure

I don't feel much sympathy for those who don't, won't, or say they can't.

Ask my friends: I can be harsh. But I'm honest. I have a low threshold for bullshit as one friend said, and I really appreciated that. I'd rather be known to be harsh and honest than soft and deceitful.

It's the unpreparedness for the truth that creates the

hurt that is felt. Maybe they'll never know the amount of effort that I put into things or the amount of pain that comes from failure. Watch a championship game in any sport and when it's over, watch the losing team. You'll see a myriad of tears, doubts, frustration, and other tragic emotions. Top athletes lose. *Then* they win. Recognize the order; the order is significant.

Tryouts: An Opportunity for Failure?

When I was in high school, tryouts were grueling. I walked into a locker room after nine intense days of hot weather, track work, hills, suicides, and small-sided games. The coach sat 50 hopefuls down and looked us over sternly. His beer belly hung over his shorts, his shirt was sweaty, his hat covered his brow, and his sunglasses concealed his intent.

He was intimidating.

"These players made varsity. If I call your name, go sit over there. After I'm done, Coach will call the JV squad out. Those names not called can go home. We don't have room for everyone, but come out next year after some hard work." That was it. Done. Decided and delivered in 17 seconds.

Today, we soften the blow for players and families, parents take on the responsibility of manipulating the results of tryouts as if players are *supposed* to be on a certain team (often because of their sense of entitlement), and the political landscape of the game has drastic effects on success.

In May each year, the soccer program I coach for hosts tryouts for the following fall, winter, and spring seasons. If you enjoy the coaching aspect of the game (developing talent, educating youth about the sport, and enriching their whole person), then you probably hate tryouts.

In most environments, they are not as simple as pick and play. Let me paint a very no-nonsense image for those that imagine tryouts as a fun process where we get to hand select a team of interdependent winners.

On a regular basis, tryouts are more about parents' hurt feelings than players' defeat.

A poignant example:

I was coaching the second tier team at an accelerated club in Baltimore, and expectations were high. More than 50 players tried out, but each team could only carry 14. The top team had its roster nearly set and was only looking for a few additions or changes. I had a returning 13, but I needed to make adjustments as well. One of my players was in danger of earning very little game time. She was small, technically sound, but not as aggressive as I would have liked, especially compared to the older group. I knew she wasn't going to get the opportunity to be more aggressive in our practices. That had to come with games. Instead of emailing an offer, I called the family and told them that I'd like to move her down. Playing for another team would give her more game opportunity in which she could develop that necessary aggression plus some leadership experience. I was heartfelt about it and explained why it was important she get minutes of actual game time versus sitting for the majority of our games.

Dad was angry and inconsolable. I was cheating her. He threw out statistics from the entire season, counting things like "fifth highest goal scorer," "fourth best passing ratio," and "most frequent player to get behind the ball." He yelled profanities at me, told me I was a terrible person for doing what I had done to a poor kid.

I'm not sure where the stats came from, but as a coach of a team of ten year olds, stats are just about as important to me as knowing the number of blades of grass on the field. As you may have expected, she did not join the team, and this story happens over and over. This dad's reaction is much more common than acceptance of a decision and deep contemplation of many factors. In this case, it wasn't the kid who refused to accept evaluation. It was Dad.

In some cases, I do meet parents who graciously accept the coach's decision and explanation, and some are even in agreement. When that happens, it's not only a welcome change, it's a positive step for the child. The player must work to get back what she lost, she understands that she needs to work hard, and she sees a new environment where she can experience the other side of the coin: bottom tier verses top tier. It's an important change. Most importantly, her approach to failure is a critical building block for any athlete, and those athletes who cannot make a mistake without collapse are not built to grow.

Failing to make the team is important. Moving from one team to a less accomplished team is important. Missing that first goal is important. The player is going to take more away from that than from her parent waving the red flag to get her on the team. She's going to learn what it means to accept her level, to accept the result she earned, and to accept the heartache or disappointment. Imagine a world where we shelter our kids from all kinds of difficulties—disappointment, heartbreak, sadness. When they finally do experience them, they won't know how to cope in a healthy way. Evaluation, then, is something that should be experienced, and we caregivers need to allow it.

I learned something important when I accepted that experience. I was a player sent down. I was a player who had been cut. I was a player who was disappointed. And my parents never got in the way of that. I wanted to prove those who cut me or sent me down wrong. I wasn't whisked away to another team with some story my dad concocted to protect my feelings. It was my process to own, and I owned it all the way until I was good.

To this day, I still believe in this process.

I will fail to be good over and over until I get good.

Laissez-Faire and the Reason Youth Need Parents to Stay Quiet

I once had a phone call with a mother whose daughter had played with me for a year. In order to be moved up, the player needed to beat out a returning keeper on the top team. It wasn't just unlikely; it was impossible. The keeper was simply more agile and more experienced. The player needed lots more training than just a few hours a week with a team. If she wanted to make that leap, she had to put in some serious time on her own.

After tryouts, I told her the results and invited her to train with the top team once a week to keep her challenged. It would give her the chance for that extra training she needed if she was serious about the transition. It was the best of both worlds. And I was being honest. She wasn't ready, and it would have been a bad situation for her not having any playing time on the field, which would have been the case if I had kept her. That is no way to promote development and growth.

Tears. Then profanity. Finally aggression. In a six-minute span, I experienced the "Vicarious Meltdown." Mom went postal on me for labeling her daughter, locking her in place, and refusing to move her up to the top level team. She told me she paid a lot of money for soccer, and she deserved to have her daughter on whatever team she wanted.

The child, who had been as calm as the beach after a storm, surely saw this moment as complete catastrophe that would characterize her life from then on. I had experience dealing with upset clients through my corporate job of managing apartments, and I had this kind of communication down to a science. I knew when to explain, when to defend, and when to try to end the conversation. This was one I couldn't win.

Next was email. Words like "injustice," "crime," and "villain" powdered my inbox. I left the conversation with a swift explanation of my stance, and while my defense was morally sound, it didn't mean that I was heard. I was honest though. I rescinded my offer to the player. The team was clearly no longer a good fit for the family, and I reiterated to the mother that she was reinforcing that when her daughter didn't get what she wanted, it was acceptable to cry, yell, abuse, and demand.

This isn't a healthy response to evaluation, and it reinforces the wrong habits.

I had yearly performance reviews at my corporate job before I quit. I had job interviews. Now that I freelance and do public speaking and coaching, I am constantly evaluated. Have you ever had a manager who was a terrible example of a leader? One of my worst bosses, among her myriad flaws, constantly switched "we" and "me" in ways that were meant to conceal some pretty hefty insecurities. "We made a mistake" was a cowardly and dishonest way to call someone out, and I believe that kind of honesty to be important in business and relationships. "I organized a great project" was a selfish way to commend a team effort, especially when, as a manager, she failed to praise or acknowledge anyone else's hard work. I would share stories with my parents, looking for a little commiseration. Can you imagine what would have ensued if my parents had called her, reprimanding her for how I was treated? "Aaron is working very hard, and I think he deserves more responsibility. He is drowning in work while making you more money!" Imagine if they had acted as if I was entitled to something. Instead, they knew I would figure it out and that I needed to handle it alone. In the next 24 hours, I'd be either fired or demoted.

This hypothetical is not far from those parents who believe that they're doing right by the child by hounding a coach after a game. As caregivers, if we fail to accept honest evaluation and instead live in our ego instead of in reality, we are neither honoring our daughters' service to the sport nor being an "adult."

But these things are happening at all levels of sport. After practices, after games, between sessions, on the way to the car, to referees, to assistant volunteer coaches.

At some point, we have to stop and ask the question—if we are letting our daughters have an experience in sports, do we want her to have an experience or do we want to control an experience?

If you're upset about coaching decisions, cool off, then ask to speak to the coach one day after practice. Tell the coach the reason you'd like to talk so that they can prepare. Be respectful when you speak with them. If this is about you, and not your daughter, it's a losing battle, so be sure she's first in this. Can you implement a 24-hour rule about games? Can you, not your daughter, take the space to disconnect, to approach the conversation with more appreciation out of respect for the bigger picture? I imagine you are ready for that kind of challenge!

In an anonymous online survey, I asked my team what they liked and disliked most about being at games. They reported that they really enjoyed riding to the games with their friends. The most common thing they disliked was hearing their parents yell from the stands, regardless of whether their comments were reprimands or praise. It's embarrassing for players. If you don't remember being a young player, or if you didn't play, please know that Mom or Dad yelling from the sidelines on your behalf is embarrassing because every single comment comes across as judgement. It's even worse when your coach is on the other side of the field, away from Mom and Dad, and all you hear is deriding commentary, regardless of how that commentary was intended. Coaching from the stands is often an attempt at the parent's own self-aggrandizement rather than support or guidance for the player. If those comments are more about showing off or preventing embarrassment for the parent, the player is missing out on the love and support she needs to grow.

Ultimately, evaluation will happen in the real world. It's how we respond to it, as kids and adults, that marks how we will fare in a world that is full of people unwilling to be evaluated. More importantly, if we consider how daughters will model our behavior, what is the example we are setting when we get honest feedback, learn the truth, or are tested and shown to be short?

Failure to let your kid fail will create two things, both of which I've seen DESTROY players. Her confidence will not be built on anything solid; instead, its foundation will be lofty lies, dreams, and the parent's over-inflated ego. Eventually, that bubble will burst, and the player will leave the sport or the parent will blame the coach and pull the kid from the team. Additionally, the false praise eventually leads the kid to believe that praise comes without action, derailing my commentary as a coach and untying the knot between hard work and progress. Neither is worth the long term effects on a kid.

As I've learned and grown to respect, young women are capable of handling much of what is thrown at them. Are we capable of leading them from "handling" to "learning?"

ACTION STEPS FOR THIS CHAPTER

Building Perspective: If you are reaching out to coaches with complaints, issues, and problems, ask yourself these questions:

- *Is the conversation I'm about to have an attempt to shield my daughter from any kind of evaluation?*
- *Is the issue at hand a result of an evaluation? Is it one that comes from a place of honesty?*
- *Is there some lesson that could be extracted from this experience my daughter is having that would prepare her for real world events?*

- *How can I exemplify how to deal with evaluation, and what conversation would show her I support her even when it's not the outcome she may have wanted?*

- *Can this event create a dialogue about what may be necessary to grow to a point where this evolution is seen as a good reminder of what's needed to be successful?*

CHAPTER 2

Acceptance: The Beautiful Connection and the Destructive Cancer

"Let us always meet each other with a smile,
for the smile is the beginning of love."
Mother Teresa

We used to play this game as a kid and now it's a regular practice drill.

Coach would set up cones in a square, and one person would be "it." When they tagged another person, they had to link hands and do everything together. It was a game that was so simple—can you avoid the growing snake and be the last person standing. If the snake broke hand-lock, anyone in it had to do 25 pushups. The drill wasn't just for fun and getting loose, the drill was about leadership, and a group working together to achieve something.

Most of the time, the snake would break as players on opposite ends had their own agenda, fervently swiping to try to tag players near them, then casting blame and shame around when the chain broke. If the snake communicated and selected one target and didn't stop until that person got tagged, it never mattered whether there were 5 players in the chain or 16.

I have worked for companies that felt like a broken chain. Blame was part of the culture.

Sometimes we don't click with our work environment or classmates or teammates, but that doesn't have to be accepted as normal. This chapter is about understanding how we caregivers influence athletic environments and the ways we caregivers can influence those environments positively.

Competition: The Double-Edged Sword

Despite what most would think, the way your team interacts is directly influenced by both parents and coaches and the messages both send the players. It's important we talk about the positive and negative connections among players on teams of young women and how you and those around your daughter influence them. How do we actively engage a team in ways that make players want to unify? To me, that's always been simple. Maybe not easy, but simple. And it all boils down to communication and messaging.

Growing up in our current social climate, girls face unique and unprecedented challenges: They've got to be everything—strong yet gentle, aggressive but welcoming, beautiful *and* intelligent. Societal standards exacerbate the very thing that binds a team together: competition. That competitive spirit among team members is one thing, while competition among individuals is another. It walks closely with jealousy.

Competition begets success in any team environment, but when it becomes too personal, it erodes team progress. I remember being awestruck by the talented group of players around me one year. We'd take the title, no question. As the season progressed, we all knew that the unity and collaboration we enjoyed at the season's start had imploded, and now all we could hope for was getting over ourselves. We had major issues with acceptance.

To address this, I would have to get more open and more raw. I set up a team meeting and did my best to create a safe space for sharing. I was vulnerable, offering that I'd failed to create the right environment for the girls and that I was worried that they didn't like each other because of the way I had been running things.

I prompted them to share their thoughts and experiences, which went incredibly well. I hoped my purpose in holding this meeting was obvious: establishing a completely open environment where discussion of our failings might get heated but would eventually cool to a strengthened layer of molten rock rather than a disconnected pile of loose stones with no foundation. Dissent among the team, along the sidelines, and among various cliques characterized the meeting as it had characterized the whole year. It wasn't as simple as "starters" versus "bench." It was a complicated system of like-minded individuals—parents and players both—who couldn't form a collective, even though they all acknowledged a shared purpose. There wasn't a unifying factor to be found anywhere.

Ultimately, it didn't work.

It was a strong effort, but the platform that the team was built on was crumbling, and no matter what paint we applied to the house, it wasn't a stable structure.

I had failed to get everyone on board and create consistent messaging. So parents were fueling the fire while we met to put it out. I would hear comments after games about how "[So-and-so] should have passed you the ball, you were open in front of goal that one time." It wasn't constructive or helpful and ultimately, it thwarted anything we built at the meeting.

It's part of what prompted this book. How could I create an atmosphere where we were all on the same page, where parents understood the outcomes of the sport experience and could then support it?

One of the biggest outcomes was learning to work on a team, whether or not you're the biggest, bestest friend of someone. Because, let's be honest, that's how 100% of the working world is.

Here's what I've learned. If you build a team and don't consider that parents are a part of that team and are influencing players nearly as much as a coach would, then you're going to eventually feel the outcome of whatever messages parents are sending. If they are positive, the outcomes are positive. If they are negative, well, good luck.

Coaches have a significant role in all of this, of course. They are the CEOs of their team and should therefore be communicating effectively to all parties. But I got some tough lessons that year, and it all boiled down to this:

I failed to give parents the tools to relay the same messages I was sending to the girls at practice.

The plus side of having a new team each season is that I get to try new systems and approaches. The next season I tried something new. I gave parents tools. I outlined things to say on the sidelines and things I shouldn't hear. I shared the team culture with them and got their buy-in. I got them to believe in what we were doing. Three families left after that meeting. They said they "wanted to be on a team where winning came first."

Woah.

Winning is a byproduct of culture.

And within the bounds of culture are all the lines of communication needed to be successful. If a player cannot accept a teammate, there is a single strand loss. If a parent cannot accept a teammate, there are two strands of loss—one from the parent and one from the results of bad-mouthing to a player so the player believes it as well.

When armed with a simple outline, the rules, expectations, consequences, options, and tactics from both parents and players, the team flourished. Did we win everything—no. We'll talk about how you never want to win everything later. We grew, and those girls on that team got to be a part of a team that supported them and whose parents supported them, a team where they could be themselves and feel safe.

The basics of those pillars were this:

- **EARNINGS:** Players shall be rewarded for effort, grit, growth, skill, commitment, and communication. Nothing is offered without being competitive and earning it. There are no free lunches and no parental or other influence will change the way player earning is counted.

- **NOISE**: Be loud—share lots of praise and positivity for effort and grit.

- **ACCEPTANCE**: No bad-mouthing other players, on or off the field.

- **COACHING**: No coaching (advice) from the sidelines unless you want to be on the staff and show up to practices, games, and run them.

- **ISSUES**: If you have an issue, please reach out to me or email me to set up a time to talk directly. If your daughter has an issue, please have her talk to me alone unless your presence is directly related to the issue.

- **PRIORITY**: The team comes before an individual. The player's responsibility is to the team, not to pleasing mom or dad.

- **GOALS**: What does she want? What *she* wants should become your targets, not the other way around. It's not her job to fulfill your goals (college, scholarship, next level, or whatever).

- **RESULTS**: The team is measured by the ability to win. The player is measured by her ability to grow and to contribute. The parent is measured by their ability to support a player in reflection and growth. The coach is measured by how all parts support the whole.

Inside of that team culture is a high degree of competition. You have to earn it. Girls competed against each other in ways that would make most people uncomfortable. But when it was all said and done, it was back to being on the same team.

When I look back at that, the success of that culture was not just fostering an acceptance among players and parents. It was creating the guidelines for both parents and players to live inside of the competitive bubble. Once invited in, and given the proper boundaries and accountability to those boundaries, everyone could reap the benefits of the collective.

Anything else and we were just a string of people all trying to go our own direction, even if that meant usually becoming untethered and failing.

Without competition that's healthy, it's impossible to raise a team. We need to be able to compete, to fail, to get measured, and be shown our weaknesses and flaws. We must consistently return to the gridiron to challenge what we know ourselves to be. And when it does not go well and when players do not do things right, instead of looking at them and condemning them with some ego-driven commentary about what they should and shouldn't have done in relationship to a daughter you care for deeply, we should instead give players the space to reflect and learn from the experience.

This requires deep self-reflection from you. Are you the poison and toxic parent on the sidelines? Are you whispering distrust during the car ride or from the practice field? Are you subjecting your player to disbelieving the coach or the team?

If you have trouble answering that because you're not clear, reread the pillars above and work to embody them yourself. You are on the same ship with the coach, the players, and the other parents.

It is because we accept the team that there is a team. Good, bad, or ugly. We're all in this together. I guess you'd better start working toward the team goal—basketball, soccer, martial arts, you name it.

Building the Path to Acceptance with Conscious Conversation

There are so many things that can divide us. Some youth will have rich parents and may not understand what others don't have, some will be very verbal, some will be tentative, and some will have confidence. My job is to highlight things that they all share and to use that to push the team forward together. You can help support this at home too, and if you avoid the pitfalls described in this chapter, you'll be creating a deep culture of acceptance around your daughter that will deepen her connection to her team, regardless of the competition.

The message underlying all communication among parents, coaches, and players is that the whole is more valuable than any individual, and the whole is better with you in it.

Over the years, I've witnessed that conversations we parents and coaches have with our youth are riddled with our own egos rather than being constructive discussions focused on the player. Often, we seem unable to disconnect *our* past wants, needs, and fears from the expectations we have from our daughters.

Most notable pain point: Coaches or parents who talk about what *they* did or didn't do in relation to what their player/daughter is pursuing. Showing that you are comfortable with what you did or did not accomplish through sports gives your daughters space to achieve to their capacity rather than the responsibility of filling your void.

Here's a great question to ask if you're unsure how you feel about that point. Are you happy with the way your athletic career turned out? If yes, great. Shut up about it. If not, great, move on from it and keep your daughter out of that process. Time after time I am working with players who think that they are exempt from hard work because their parent accomplished something, or the exact opposite, they are working hard because they want to live up to what their parent accomplished.

Neither is healthy. If acceptance truly does start at home, it starts with our language.

Imagine a player hearing from her coach or a parent that her teammate "is really bad" or "isn't ready for this level." What would you expect her to mirror in her actions or to repeat? We repeat what we hear or repeat what we think we know. It's common to repeat hearsay as fact, especially when the source is credible, but as influencers of our youth, we must be careful what we mutter.

I've had a bad game. Haven't you?

In conversations with your daughter about other players who didn't have a great game or who need to develop skills:

- Steer the conversation to how your daughter could help those players build those skills. Remind her that a game is played with 11 team members, and one player can only play her best; she can't be the whole team.

- Steer the conversation toward how she might better assist the team. What can she control?

- Steer the conversation toward those people who would be able to help the team find a way to close the gap. Have her talk to Coach about it.

That's not to say that all teams are made equal.

There are times where players may need to shift teams. A team change or level change, up or down, doesn't need to be a bad thing. There are players at all levels, and when you remove the ego from the conversation, the team change is likely best for your daughter.

Problems arise in how we talk about team change. I know parents who have thrown temper tantrums at this concept. Full grown men and women, yelling and stamping their feet because the team isn't the right fit for their player. You would think I stabbed someone they love.

Parents, it's when you believe that she won't ever ______________________________ (insert a goal that you installed for her) if she makes this move or when you worry about what other people think, or worse yet, when you assume that she'll be unhappy and tell her that team is for ____________ (losers, new players, or whatever derogatory term you use) that your conversation becomes toxic.

In my career I've taken dozens of players from an upper team and welcomed them. When they had the right parental conversation around it, all parties were happy. In fact, about 40% of those players eventually moved back up to higher levels—because as we'll talk about, enjoying the game and understanding the process inside a culture of acceptance breeds success.

"Psychological safety is the shared belief that the team is safe for interpersonal risk-taking."

Amy Edmondson

Fostering Acceptance through Leadership

We all crave psychological safety, no matter the environment, and the foundation of that safety is acceptance.

Like everyone else, girls create hierarchies within team structures. Unfortunately, bullying and hazing are not uncommon, but we caregivers can provide players with tools to foster positive leadership with new or struggling team members.

When a player is frustrated, it's condescending to stop practice to isolate her. I can't always step away to work with a player one-on-one, so I rely on my players to uplift each other. I pull a top player to the side, share my expectations, my request, and walk them through how they could do it. If my expectations are appropriately high, they can lead without me—without my nudge. The more a skilled player works with a struggling player, the better both of them get. It's scientific knowledge that teaching improves the skill more quickly than anything else, so that makes sense. However, it also sends a ripple through the team: *The gap between top players and bottom players doesn't exist. The hierarchy you allowed to develop and separate you doesn't exist.* Players have to struggle, but they don't have to struggle alone.

As coaches, we should bear in mind that our sense of leadership may be too limited. We think of it as the "leader" and the "led," but effective leadership has several different forms. We all notice the leader who yells directions. We don't necessarily notice the player who leads by example or the player who is quietly influencing others with quiet, constructive guidance. To think that your daughter is not a leader because she is not a captain is to account for only one type of leadership. Do not make the mistake of thinking she cannot lead.

The acceptance necessary for success starts with the acceptance of all leaders around a young lady. Are you accepting of who is a part of your team? Are you demonstrating that you are supportive to what is around the team and what your daughter is doing with her athletic career?

Similarly, allowing our young athletes to be the leaders, empowering them to do things their way, and to look at those still learning and developing as athletes with potential and not with deficits, we give way to acceptance at a larger level.

Opportunities: Fostering Acceptance as a Caregiver

When I asked one player what she wished her parents wouldn't do and she wrote, "Compare me to other players when I would have an 'off' game or just a bad game in general."

One of the most intimidating things I heard when I first started coaching girls was that I should "be careful because girls can be very cliquey." Girls *can* be cliquey, but so can boys, and so can adults, and so can bears, for that matter. It's natural for people with like minds and traits to flock together. That's not the problem. The cancer of fragmentation on a team really originates when those minds and traits collide and conflicting beliefs surface, and that is where you come in as a caregiver.

Some common denominators among team members create strong bonds, and some create bonds that are much weaker. Without strong bonds, a team cannot truly overcome toxicity or negativity. Those weak ones will solidify bonds, but they typically don't have enough power to create them. A team needs enough bonding to ensure that everyone is included; otherwise, the team operates inefficiently. Imagine a typewriter (yes, I said "typewriter") on which the levers on the "E" and "A" keys don't function; your words, and therefore your messages, are limited by those levers' operations. Your daughter is among a team that is the same way: Strong bonds create a team environment where every player is accepted. The exclusion of even one member means your team's message doesn't convey.

The need for connectivity is visible on teams that have poor chemistry. You'll see its symptoms in times of trouble, not necessarily in times of success, but players will bicker on field, blame others, point fingers, lash out about mistakes, and condemn a second string player for getting on the field when a first string player sits on the bench. Things of that nature indicate that it's time to address behaviors at home.

FACTORS THAT CREATE STRONG BONDS	FACTORS THAT CREATE WEAKER BONDS
Feelings toward a coach (anger, frustration, fear, or respect, etc.)	Love of the game
Game results	Parental pressure
Goals or objectives	Individual performances or praise
Overcoming obstacles and defeat	Other common interests
Praise of team's off-field shared experiences	Club affiliation
	Shared professional player favorites

Acceptance is a goal for the long term, but steps can be taken in the short term to invest in your team's future as a whole collective unit—namely by working with your daughter. I've seen a team of girls go from a shortlisted, developmentally-capable-but-emotionally-unstable, underperforming team to a congealed, over-performing, cross-functional unit in a matter of weeks. The core of that change came from creating an environment where players make deep connections with each other, one in which those connections were reinforced among all levels of the team (captain, first string, second string, and keepers). You can foster much of that at home.

Creating Strong Bonds (or "Misery Creates Company")

My 2014 team serves as an apt example of how to create strong bonds. That year, many players returned from the previous year, but a fair number of them would be outmatched by some of the new players. Earning playing time was a critical component of my strategy for team unity, so it was important that I unite them on one common plane quickly: Through their collective distaste for the hard work and heartache I required of them in practice came a bond that created the level playing field and unity I desired. Only working together would they bond, and the fastest way to get them there was to give them a common enemy. After only a few practices, they understood that I was going to be the bad guy who would require them to complete the most challenging drills these players had seen. I set out to challenge their minds and their bodies, and through that, the conversation they would have among themselves would focus on something consistent.

I began their training with a 15-minute two-mile run. Players who didn't make it had to run an extra lap at a different but still challenging pace. If they found a teammate to replace them on the punishment lap, I would allow it, but if the replacement player did not make it, they both had to run again. When practices started, they all commiserated over the ensuing pain, but it got them in a small circle—all of them together. They attempted to guess the next set of workouts, shared horror stories from last practice, and reproached my coaching style. I loved it! It gave us a great platform for banter, challenges, bets, and commentary, and it forced the entire team to fight through something together, persevere, and sacrifice themselves for the survival of a teammate. That alone hit on two bonding opportunities: overcoming obstacles and feelings toward a coach.

An Amazing Thought about Events

If there's one thing I've learned coaching girls, it's that a team event that creates team chemistry is just as valuable as, if not more than, a really intense training session. Help your coach by offering to organize team activities like trips to trampoline parks, rope climbing, dodgeball, and family dinners. It is one thing to have a team that comes together to conquer the coach's challenges twice a week, but it's another to have players who want to hang out with each other outside of training. There's little likelihood they would elect to organize an event for the whole team on their own initially, but with a good push in the right direction and some momentum to build acceptance, you can create chemistry through these activities. If someone doesn't believe it will create value, buy them this book.

My team members and even some of their parents joined the ColorRun. While we didn't get full attendance, we did have a full team conversation about it and even placed wagers on race times. We also worked with Applebee's to host several pancake breakfasts as fundraisers. The players invited friends and family by selling tickets and were responsible for serving food and bussing tables at the event. It wasn't a major time commitment or a financial burden, but the fact that they had to work together for the team and to mitigate expenses (which most parents are all about) meant that we were able to solidify some of what's needed to be successful on the field—operate together for a common goal. Encourage your team to take on these roles, and you'll be shocked at how much it can foster amazing conversations.

Here are some ideas for you to consider as you look at team events:

- Trampoline parks
- Bowling
- Indoor skydiving
- Clue rooms
- Laser tag
- Dinners and lunches
- Athletic events (professional games, in person or on TV)
- Athletic challenges (ninja courses, 5Ks)
- Charity events and volunteering
- Fundraisers

Coach's Corner: Carrots, Sticks, and Follow-through

Imagine that you are at your full-time job reporting to your boss about a completed assignment. If you complete a task on time, your boss thanks you, but if you submit it two hours early, he gives you an extra half hour for lunch. If you fail to complete an assignment on time, you are docked four hours of pay. You have both a carrot and a stick to motivate you. One is to move you toward the desirable behavior and one to move you away from the less desirable behavior. Propelled by this combination, you are performing as you should, completing items on time or early. Then, you slip. You turn in an assignment late, and you report to your boss as usual. Instead of docking you, he tells you that you've been performing excellently, and that he will not dock your pay. You got away with it!!! Whew!

A week later, you slip again, and again, you're not docked. Now the propellant has started to deflate and become less effective as you no longer respect that kind of negative consequence. You might understand that there is a benefit to working extra hard, but like water, you find the path of least resistance, work just as much as is needed, and experience no penalty for not completing assignments on time. The more frequently it happens, the less power the stick has and the less benefit the carrot offers. So you escape to your mediocrity.

As a coach, your carrot is your team's success. It's important that you recognize and accentuate that in front of the team. "When we do this right, we will win games," is enough. You can mix in results and comments about playing the right way, being stronger or faster, or earning a title. Regardless, the carrot should be standard for the team. I've used the carrot of playing time often in my career. "The players that do this better will earn more time."

Whatever tactic you decide to employ, *do not forget your words*. Your team won't. I'm shocked at how much my girls remember and how important it is that I stick to my word. It's how they evaluate whether or not a person is trustworthy. If punishments must fall on your best player right before the toughest game of the season, you must enforce them. If there are players who will never be able to complete a punishment, force them to either push through it or find a suitable replacement. Failure to follow through on a promised reward or consequence will create an environment of manipulation where players will take advantage of emotions, situations, and other variables to mitigate the punishment. If an alternative needs to be given, give one that is equal in measure, so that they must make a tough decision. The more resolute you are and the more concrete your rules seem, the more of a boundary you create and the more respect you can generate. It is often better to be consistently harsh than occasionally mean. It's an expectation and standard that we create when we are consistent.

If they clearly understand the consequences and rewards of any behavior, it's easy to support the correct one and encourage them to demonstrate it more consistently. Sir Alex Ferguson, one of the most successful football coaches in Europe, was known for saying but two words to encourage his players: "Well done." It doesn't need to be lavish or excessive, but it should be consistent. When you use the carrot and the stick successfully, you will ultimately have a team that is unified in its response to you. When you tell them what you expect in a drill, you'll have their attention and you'll capture their energy. If you have not established your parameters successfully, you'll lose them to distraction, conversation, or even worse, poor performance.

At tournaments, before we leave restaurants after team meals, I tell the girls to "sweep" to make sure there aren't any pieces of tableware or trash left behind. Moms go nuts for it. The magic comes from a deep rooted respect that I've built. I don't need to issue punishments, and I don't need to praise them for doing it. It's mutually understood that when they listen and respond to my requests, there is an inherent benefit. And therein lies the key point. It is simply the right thing to do, and someone they trust is expecting them to do it right. The same should apply to games. Share with them the process and when they find success, let them know. Players will trust your system when they see that it works.

When a team is unified, both parents and players can live in a space that gives everyone the courage and tolerance needed to accept the differences among players on the team. Naturally, we can find divisions in our style, level of play, learning modality, and more, but it is in this deep reflection that I'm constantly reminded that for all of our differences, we will always have more that brings us together than we have that pulls us apart.

It all starts with acceptance.

ACTION STEPS FOR THIS CHAPTER

Things to ponder at home:

- Negative talk about another player can bleed over to the way your daughter sees that player, which impacts the team. If your commentary on another player is negative, keep it to yourself.

- If you're worried about team culture, ask the coach about it. See how she or he defines it and what he or she wants out of families and players to create it. If you do this before the season starts, or during tryouts, you may prevent being on a team with toxic culture.

- Players that don't respect the athletic dynamic of a team that shares responsibility may need to be shown the importance of teamwork. Consider sharing how teamwork at your workplace affects the overall company and team. Don't worry about connecting it to soccer and making it a lecture. Just share a story of a time it went really well and a time it didn't, then ask if she thinks that same kind of thing exists on the field.

Things to reflect on:

- What is the team culture as it stands now? Is it healthy or unhealthy for my daughter's future?

- How are my actions creating or deterring acceptance? How would I rank myself at being a positive part of team culture?

- Is my language supporting other players on their individual journey or condemning them? What message does that send to my daughter?

CHAPTER 3

The Car Ride Home

"If mental abuse was a punishable crime, a lot of parents would be in jail serving a life term."

Maddy Malhotra

As I look back at my seven years of coaching nearly 200 boys and 600 girls (complete with the crazy phone calls and the aggressive emails), the moments of conflict and hostility often overshadow the good memories of successes and wins. When a parent calls or walks toward me or pulls the daughter over to me, I impulsively put a stake in the ground, pull the shield from my back, grab my spear, and prepare to defend my person, my decisions, my reasons, and my job. I hate that it is an automatic response, but it's natural. I'm most commonly attacked for a decision, comment, or an onlooker's unique perception of events.

Seasoned coaches, Bruce E. Brown (Director of *Proactive Coaching*) and Rob Miller (*Proactive Coaching* partner), through years of working with hundreds of college athletes, asked their players to recall the worst parts of their youth sports careers. Students reported that they hated the car ride home. "They were trapped in the same space as their well-intentioned parents, who couldn't help but offer ill-timed advice after the competition was over."[1] Commonly, conversations in the car on the ride home are aggressive reviews of performances, with particular focus on mistakes, missed opportunities, and inconsistencies in expectations. Parents rarely engage intending to berate and destroy the adolescent mind and undo the constructs of confidence. It's done with love and hope and all the things we say to make ourselves feel better as leaders of young women. I've done it wrong myself many times. Intentions aside, athletes are opening up and admitting more frequently that they detest these moments. Parents are commonly forcing them to relive the least successful moments of the game as if a young athlete is ignorant of her own mistakes (and as if a coach hasn't already made her aware of her errors).

A parent's knee-jerk reaction is, "My kid would never say that she hated riding home with me," or "That advice is for those crazy parents. I'm not one of them."

---

[1] *Woodward, H., "One simple way to stop criticizing your youth athlete on the car ride home," Maternal Media, October 24, 2015. Retrieved January 07, 2018, from* **https://maternalmedia.com/2015/10/24/one-simple-way-to-stop-criticizing-your-youth-athlete-on-the-car-ride-home/**

However, studies show that kids, like adults, are likely to skew answers if they feel that truth will negatively affect them. Ask any successful business owner why he/she uses a *third party* to survey employee or client satisfaction. Trapped in a car with her parents, a girl is unlikely to share feedback that's 100% open and honest. Why would she? She is likely to be judged, chastised, and reprimanded. Instead, she may retreat into the safety of silence.

During halftime one game, I posed a question to the group of girls on the sideline. We were at a light-hearted scrimmage and mixing groups. Pressure was off. Some of them were recovering from injury too.

"What's the worst thing you've ever heard your parents say on the sideline?" I asked.

"Sideline?!? You should be in the car after the games."

Recently I asked a few of my former and current players to do a survey about this subject. Here are comments they shared about the car ride home:

- *"I heard, 'You sucked today.'"*
- *"My parents have said that I wasn't trying and that I needed to try harder (when I felt like I was doing my best)."*
- *"I wish parents would understand that we as female athletes are already under constant pressure: from our male peers, teammates, teachers, coaches,*

and sometimes even from ourselves, because living in a world where women's sports are not viewed to be as competitive as men's inherently forces us to work harder."

- *"It would help if they knew that sometimes players have bad games and that's just the way it is. We are always trying even if we just have a bad performance sometimes."*

What are the chances this is happening in your car?

Put Yourself in Your Daughter's Shoes

Visualize the beginning of a beautiful day. You are eager to get to your awesome, kick-ass, high-paying, fulfilling job. Today is the day you make your prowess clear to your company's managers. Today is the day you will make a speech in front of leadership, presenting your plan for the next two years of operations—the numbers, the timeline, the team. Your boss leaned on you to perform, and it's the day you've been waiting for.

Your hands grip the steering wheel with confidence, your boss is in the passenger seat, and you have a good sense of his excitement and expectations for your upcoming presentation about a big project proposal. You have reviewed the presentation in detail with your boss, and he gave you encouraging feedback. He didn't say it explicitly, but there's a promotion on the line. You can feel it. You could be the head of the whole developing launch!

You walk into the presentation room, your audience awaits, and you can feel that this win is in the script based on your significant time investment and the buzz about you in company emails. Feeling prepared, you load your presentation and eye the prize: exuberant applause and resounding recognition of your esteemed intellect and technical understanding. Later: the title, the parking spot, the raise. A senior executive introduces you. "Exciting new talent," he says. "Refreshing and bright employee here to present . . ." The podium glows, gracefully inviting you into its wide, wooden embrace. As you're called to it, you set your palms, a moist depiction of your anxiety, onto the podium and look down at the computer. The steady lights match your heart rate: calm, controlled. You got this.

Wait. Something's wrong. Your heart rate starts to rise. Where is the flash drive that you brought in earlier? *It was here.* Sweat builds. It takes an eternity to find your spare flash drive. Sixty seconds lapse, and already the corporate audience is fidgeting. Three minutes of fumbling feels like another eternity, and your boss comes over to try to calm you down. Instead, his slew of questions raises your heart rate to a panic. "Just get this moving. I saw you with it. Where did you put it?" As if that's helpful now.

After your 10-minute presentation, you know you messed up. You lost your grip on the material and the delivery cadence. A lukewarm applause prompts your immediate exit and grumbles mixed with indignant laughter follow you out. You walk off in defeat, and the humid air in the hallway meets your lungs like rolling tides on an empty beach, slapping and flattening your energy. You make the fastest escape possible. Comrades try to give you moral support, but their encouragement falls on deaf ears. Regardless of what they say, you know you blew it. You make it to your car, sweating, panting. *Failure.*

Your self-talk at this point sounds more like an enemy than normal.

You drop your head on the steering wheel, hands beneath your seat with car door wide open. "Why didn't you just take the drive up there with you instead of trying to get ahead of the curve?" Words can be weapons. And your boss's, as he resumes his place in the passenger's seat, seem like flaming napalm catapulted into straw cities. You disassociate, eyes dejectedly staring elsewhere. Before long, your boss's incessant declarations become permanent scars, and the drive home only serves to recycle the negative energy inward, fueling the smolder of your self-worth, confidence, and commitment. It's a landslide.

You. Can't. Escape.

Neither can she.

It's all too common for parents to eviscerate their own daughter during the car ride home. If you are in fact guilty of badgering the witness in a locked, moving vehicle where there's no escape, you are probably unaware of what you are putting your loved one through. We are disconnected and have myopic tendencies, but these tendencies are like wrecking balls to the pillars of confidence and developing players.

One player said this in a survey about what they wish their parent never would have done:

> *If I get in the car and you're thinking I've had a bad game, trust me: I already know, and I'm more upset over it than you are. It's not helpful for you to tell me what to do better. Especially with a few coaches I had, I had a period where I would be in constant fear of failure. I was in such fear of failure that I would fail. I could never play to what I knew was the best of my ability because I was so terrified that I would perform poorly.*
>
> *Then, if I made a mistake, I would be unable to move past that, and it would further impact my playing. I got stuck in a cycle of "I'm not good enough; I've never been good enough; I never will be good enough." I had those thoughts running on repeat through my head in some games. It was terrible. To feel that way, and then get in the car and hear "You know, you didn't have your best game. Next time, I think you should . . ." is incredibly difficult. By the time I'm in the car after the game, I've already run every mistake I made back through my head and agonized over it.*
>
> *It was a huge impediment to me as an athlete, and although I've begun to work past it, I still struggle. It sounds like such a trivial thing, but it's hugely impactful.*

The following five tools include insights that you might be blind to because of your affection, pride, and emotional attachments. Sometimes your energy is the enemy, so it is important to address the actions you might be taking and alter them so that they align with your child's future. Keep an open mind about these tools, regardless of whether or not you are good at communicating with your child. Read them as though you are learning how to capitalize on an amazing opportunity. You can always improve your ability to connect with your daughter, and this is something your daughter needs from you. In pursuit of your own affirmation of power or authority, is it possible you're not entirely cognizant of what's on the receiving end of your communication?

I. Don't be your daughter's fan

Have you read the Tweets fans post to the accounts of their favorite athletes? Fans are critical. Fans are cruel. Fans are trivial and fickle. Fans base feelings on wins and losses. Fans burn jerseys. I'm asking you *not to be her fan*.

Your daughter needs you to be her escalator, the mechanism that circles her from underneath and carries her up, regardless of whether she is tired and defeated or praised and joyful. Moments most prone to empower kids tend to become traps, uphill battles against the people they hold in high esteem and who should be their keepers, safeguarding their identities. Instead of being empowered, daughters are often left feeling like you when your boss chewed you out. The car ride home offers you an opportunity to instill in your daughter a growth mindset model. Navigating this opportunity to speak, share, and converse can be significantly challenging. I asked one of my players, "What's it like? Does he yell at you when you get in the car?" She said, "He doesn't yell. He just tells me what I did wrong. I'm used to it now."

That a child would simply accept the fact that she is miserable without contesting the source of the pain is more alarming than would be an aggressive outburst. Doesn't this behavior mimic that of abuse victims? Lowered self-esteem, acclimation to suffering, and disconnection from the symptoms. Is this well-meaning father's focus on what the kid was missing or what he assumed the kid missed? How fixated are we on solving a problem only we see, addressing a need that is uniquely ours, and preventing harm to us? If that is the focus of the conversation in the car on the way home, we undermine the very fabric that makes our kids strong. And we miss a great opportunity.

Passivity is an undervalued aspect of coaching and parenting and of leading. We think of leaders as warriors like Napoleon, riding on an aggressive stallion, galloping into musket fire. Or Leonidas, spear in hand against the onslaught of Persians. We don't think of leadership as silent and passive, but steering winds have always guided ships destined for great discovery, even though those winds were silent. So, as a reminder: You don't need to know more than your daughter. That's the coach's job. To make her the best person she can be, she'll need you to be more than a fan.

What would our athletes accomplish if we started to better lead them? Where would that new height be? In leading someone to find her own version of awesome, being her fan means you take controlling actions. You yell, gripe, protest, barter away in your fantasy league, and "boo" after a bad call or coaching decision. She deserves leadership that empowers her to move forward, not a chain tied to her neck that pulls her forward based on someone else's decision.

Don't be her fan. She deserves better.

II. Build a feedback loop

The first time I was told I wouldn't be able to play soccer again, I cried. In fact, I wept uncontrollably. Eventually, I started to ask questions that changed my life. Now I ask the same questions after each failure and each success. They are open-ended questions, such as "What's next?" "How come . . . ?" and "What if . . . ?"

Successful individuals understand how to employ what's called a feedback loop, a cycle of evaluations after each success and failure. It's an asset to a successful person, and it's replicated time and time again. By creating an environment where exploration is *your daughter's* goal, not *your* goal, you will enable her to share her thoughts and cement her own lesson. For an athlete or an entrepreneur, the feedback loop should be a simple series of questions that is intentional, sometimes tough, and forward-thinking. The process should feel engaging, even fun. "What does it feel like to me?" It's taking a session, a game, or a conversation and stopping for a moment to say, "How can I do that better? What can I take away from that to improve this experience next time?" It's an individual timeline that requires the right mental state: one that is non-emotional and non-combative.

I've seen two types of feedback loops employed. One creates success, and the other suppresses it. Creating a proper mindset in our athletes requires careful language. The two approaches often differ by only a single word. One asks, "Why did you . . . ?" while the other screams, "Why didn't you . . . ?" One posits, "How would you . . . ?" while the other scolds, "Why would you . . . ?" *By employing a language shift, we can train our athletes to disengage from an emotionally charged moment because the post-game reflection offers the best opportunity for deep learning.* Closed-ended questions make for short, passive-aggressive answers. "Didn't you see that coming?" "She was wide open; didn't you hear her?" Because they can be answered with a "yes" or "no," questions like these are more reprimand than opportunity for discussion. If a player can answer in less than two words, you dropped the ball—not her.

Frequently, we assert our dominance by stifling conversation and guiding it back to us as the experts or advisors. It makes us feel needed. But dependency is not the objective; her freedom and confidence are. If we adults are really there to listen, why is it so often that we choose to validate our authority by asking questions that are both obvious and derogatory?

Consider using growth perspective terminology, basing future opportunity on consistent forward progress *versus* a fixed one, basing a result on an aspect of personality or ability that is unchangeable. Ask questions that help her see the never-ending loop of input, output, and review. For example:

GROWTH	FIXED
"I could work on . . . "	"I'm bad at . . . "
"Next time I could . . . "	"I should have . . ."
"I wish I knew why . . . "	"I hate when . . . "

The feedback loop, with proper language and open-floor-conversation, can transform a loss into a positive experience, which is the moment where athletes at top levels really shine. This is how you can let her shine.

III. Encourage open-ended dialogue

Does your daughter seem to be disinterested in talking about the game? Does she respond in mono-syllables? Does she mischaracterize the whole thing as "good" or "bad"? Then stop talking about the game. Talk about the weather. Dinner. Pokémon. Asphalt. ANYTHING. JUST NOT THE GAME. This way, you can unlock a few doors to see if she is ready to share, but the bottom line is, **if your daughter does not want to talk about the game, don't talk about it.**

I loved learning how Will Smith and his wife, Jada Pinkett-Smith, discipline their kids, or better yet, how they don't. When they observe behaviors that are "unwelcome" in their household or which make them uncomfortable as parents, rather than yelling, screaming, and kicking down doors, they place the opportunity for positive dialogue squarely at the feet of the child by asking, "Why was what you did right?" This approach forces critical thinking, analysis, and communication without any direct pressure. Is there implied pressure? Sure. We are challenging them to prove their case, creating connections between cause-and-effect for both themselves and others. But it's innocent-until-proven-guilty. If they aren't ready to share, *they* think about it. Isn't that what we want our young women to be able to do?

Similar to the situation with the car ride home, this approach assumes that the conversation is initiated and fulfilled by the authority figure. However*, we are building the habits of being kid-centric and therefore should consider that the origin of the conversation should be the kid, not us. We are merely shepherding her toward self-discovery***.**

Consider that most kids will do the opposite of what you want them to do. Ask them to brush their teeth daily or wear a belt, and see what you get. Good luck. Contradictory to our logic, they operate most effectively in communication when we make it clear that they are welcome to share when they feel like sharing, not when we make them feel that sharing is a prerequisite for love and support.

Welcome her into conversation with open arms and guide her to arrive at clear realizations that are best for her overall development. This task will require you to listen more than speak and to avoid speaking if she is not speaking. If you need to vent, call someone during the game. If you don't have that someone who will listen to you rant about your 12-year-old daughter's soccer game and how she's the next Mia Hamm, take the hint and shut up. To allow your daughter space to speak is to empower her toward her next challenge. The moment you speak, you dismiss her need to share and exist in that moment. Instead, begin the conversation with an open-ended and delicate question. Let silence be, and encourage communication by being prepared to listen.

If she is ready and willing to talk, here are a few places to begin:

- *How do you feel about your performance today?*
- *What did you learn today?*
- *What would you do differently?*
- *What was your personal (or team) highlight?*
- *What do you need to work on?*
- *What could you practice now that would have made that game better?*
- *Where was your best action? Where was your worst?*

Notice that these are all open-ended questions. They allow someone to wander where they feel comfortable and disclose what they feel safe sharing. Proceed without recourse if what you hear doesn't align with what you think you want to hear. It's not about you. Listen closely. When you can listen carefully and consistently, you'll guide the conversation in the right direction, and you'll be amazed at the realizations that present themselves. Watching a young girl have a moment of insight is awesome, even if she's not your daughter. She is the origin of a wonderful energy and beautiful opportunity—don't squander it with your dispossession.

IV. Destroy the magnitude of this moment

At the end of each competition lies the beginning of the next. If we criticize our future Olympians, professional athletes, businesswomen, scientists, and leaders about their present performance, how are we empowering their next endeavor? Are we empowering them at all?

"Preparation" suggests that you're solely focused on what's to come. As I build my businesses, write a book, learn about coaching, develop better a sense of self, I've learned that preparation is being present—learning to be comfortable with *what is* and really living in that moment. Yet living in the moment often means debunking the myth of the moment's grandeur. It's not the most important game ever, and perhaps this isn't the most important book I will ever write. By living in the present and removing the weight of a sliver of time, you encourage players to be engaged in this moment, not the ones that are now in the past. While the feedback loop enables someone to see ahead, this alteration allows them to see *now* as a part of that growth, not as the antithesis to it.

Some of my players think that losing a game is the end of their career. In turn, I help them focus on using those open-ended questions. I use the same process on separate occasions—ones in which incredible growth or success has taken place—to awaken them to the magnitude of that moment. The truest test of an athlete is consistent improvement, not one-off performances. Whether you are building skills on the tennis court, basketball court, or the pitch, yes, you are preparing for the game in the future. But if you are not present in that moment, you will not be present later.

Some of the greatest athletes have said in interviews that their youth career was all in preparation for their future. So, if it's not on a Wikipedia page or a professional record, why is it so gargantuan?

I have direct conflicts with some companies that track and score and rank teams. In soccer, it's called GotSoccer. A team of 11 year olds does not need to be ranked nationally. It places too much pressure on results over process, so teams are playing lower level teams to tally up wins rather than eyeing the process that will carry players to the next level. Rankings should not be taken seriously; in fact, I argue that these platforms have completely derailed youth sports in this country. Though I believe in measurement, these rankings are not part of that position, and in a car ride home, these should not be a part of the conversation.

To build the skill of being present without over-pressurizing the system, in the car ride home there is a need to absorb what we have *now* and be prepared to analyze and speak on behalf of our *now*. Feelings, ideas, and concepts should be allowed a safe space to live. The guiding principle is that we as adults create that safety when we listen, not when we speak.

V. Give them an escape rope

When you think about how you might better use the car ride home, the most important thing to remember is that your daughter can't escape. Entrapped in the most vile and oppressive situation, even the most noble and altruistic person can become belligerent, defensive, or apathetic. Experienced players, regardless of age, often lack the tools to manage a way out of an uncomfortable conversation. They aren't yet equipped to navigate the sweeping range of emotions. She's a kid after all. So why is our most earnest attempt at helping her improve so often a tendency to corner and pin her?

We should be able to offer an escape rope to our youth, so that they never feel defenseless. Each of us can imagine and implement apprehension-free strategies that encourage them to share their deepest thoughts without fearing our judgement. *You can employ a safe word,* or, as you build a better relationship with your daughter, feel out the situation and sense when to stop talking and change the subject. As an adult, you know how to change the subject easily and seamlessly, but your daughter hasn't mastered the ability to divert attention, so there are no conditions for dissipating the oppression she feels. Change the subject if your questions go unanswered or shift out of focus. We must always *build in a way out* for our youth. If they don't want to talk, then let silence be your conversation, turn that radio up, or select a completely new conversation subject.

ACTION STEPS FOR THIS CHAPTER

Review the questions above to help foster open-ended dialogue.

Self-reflect on these questions:

- Am I forcing conversations in the car that are being met with silence and avoidance tactics?

- Are my words critical after games? Am I placing too much of my own pride, ego, and worthiness on the results of my daughter's soccer team?

CHAPTER 4

Solitude, Self-Regulation, and Work Ethic

"Hard work beats talent when talent doesn't work hard."
Tim Notke

I've come across players who are natural dynamos—they will work their asses off in whatever arena they are placed. The other 96% of players simply will not put forth the effort in every single moment that would be required for perpetual growth and massive success. They simply don't work hard enough.

I've also started to see this in entrepreneurship since being one is now cool.

We've become increasingly soft about our notions of

hard work as a sense of entitlement continues to spread virally. And yet, there's a reality to why certain individuals continue to rise and why even the most amazing of players plateau. It takes a tremendous amount of effort, talent, hard work, and self-awareness to crack the code of average. As leaders, we must make sure our narrative of the value of hard work is consistent with our actions in order to support any goal that our young leaders have. We want our young ones to be successful and yet unscathed. We don't want them to experience our pain, yet it's our pain that drives our personality, growth, and meaning. Take away someone's pains and scars and you take away her triumph.

On several occasions, I've been asked to do more than just coach my players. Parents often want me to "change" or "motivate" their athlete as if I have some magic wand. To make a comparison, if a car is standing still, no amount of steering will change its direction. Players need to be the moving car before coaches have any impact.

As coaches, we are responsible for what gets accomplished during our session, but unfortunately, we cannot be around our players 24/7. In fact, I'm really limited. I can't do a lot for an athlete who is not motivated. I'm with them maybe a total of six hours a week with two practices and a game. Even at seven days a week, I won't approach the level of influence of all of the other people and activities in a player's life, and more importantly, all the choices they make *away* from being a great player.

We both want players to be making choices that

push them toward their best possible play, but those choices are being made at an incredible pace. Lunch, dinner, afterschool, on weekends—they all represent small choices that don't matter in the moment but add up to be hugely important in aggregate. I'm not suggesting that each and every choice a kid makes has massive consequence, or that every choice should be in support of their soccer career. I am, though, suggesting that until we realize how all of our choices add up, and how interwoven that truly is with the outcome, we tend to behave as though the success of a player lies in the hands of everyone *but* that player.

Only I am responsible for my success. Our job as caregivers is to provide the necessary environment and opportunity for a person to choose success themselves. In the world of girls' sports, we see plenty of opportunities to show athletes how to make responsible decisions, and I want to take this chapter to illustrate how small efforts on a regular basis undertaken by your daughter can rapidly accelerate her growth, deeply connect the themes needed to be successful at anything (rewards and inputs), and ground her in the reality that nothing good comes without effort.

What You Do Regularly, You Become

At any level, practices and games can only supply a portion of an athlete's total diet. The majority of teams at youth level don't or can't train every day, so it's going to be up to the youth themselves to create a regimen and a work ethic outside of, and in addition to, what you provide for them. Without it, they will not achieve their potential. No shortcuts exist, nor will they in the athletic ecosystem. Or in college. Or in a career.

Many young athletes can coast through the season with nothing but a small amount of experience and fantastic genetics. Athleticism does rule in younger age brackets (ages 10 through 16), and that natural inclination can persist even into high school. However, I see this idea of natural ability being misinterpreted often and consistently. Let's say I'm incredibly fast and agile naturally. If I'm able to use my speed and agility to dominate games, score, or create team opportunities, it is not along the "path of least resistance" for me to learn the game and learn technique. I'll just rely on my Herculean strength and speed to carry me. And carry me fast it will. I may move up to higher-level teams, but my natural gifts will not carry me much further. Top teams are full of fast and agile players. That's not what will keep me there. Skills and smarts endure.

I'm cautious of players who are purely athletic, and I monitor their understanding and development closely. They, too, must master their mind and understand the game; the alternative is a ceiling. As a coach, it's important that we recognize these players and invest in bettering their understanding of the game, which oftentimes will force you to contradict or impede their athleticism. If you're the parent of this athlete, coupling work rate and a growth mindset with their natural talent is incredibly important. For more about this, I recommend you read Carol Dweck's *The Growth Mindset*.

Emphasizing the development of players, athletic or

not, prioritizes their future, not their present. Whether a player scores 19 goals a game or none is irrelevant. Strive to arm players with the tools needed to carry them through their challenges and barriers, and no matter how naturally athletic they are, those barriers are coming. They are inevitable. Best to prepare youth for hardship by teaching them new skills. Perspective in the long term will fuel much greater success—be it in the game or outside the game.

In any sport or career, those that do something well regularly and consistently tend to rise to the top. In a world where both personal development and self-development are widely available, this also means those who are growing will get more attention. Someone willing to put in 10 minutes a day as a young adult to get better will likely have some predisposition to perform extra work when the right opportunity presents itself. It won't scare her off.

Simply being born fast or born athletic is not enough anymore, and this entire chapter is a microcosm of necessary personality traits. Those regularly willing to go above and beyond, train alone, ask questions, develop their weaknesses, identify how to achieve a goal and then add consistent action and training will be successful over the long term. It's not a secret.

It's actually very simple.

It's difficult.

But it's simple.

Solitude and Self-Regulation

I love commercials for athletic wear: Under Armour, Nike, adidas. Take a popular athlete, insert him onto a green screen, draw electricity, robots, and battle around him, and sell yourself a couple million dollars' worth of product. The recipe, though, is flawed from its ingredients to its delivery. The attractiveness of an athlete to youth is built on things that aren't real, and even more problematically, is built on things that can't be bought, traded, bartered, or colored in.

When I have conversations with my team members about their goals as individuals or with their families, I find that most of my players aim to play in high school or college. Some are ready, and some are not; regardless, I use the opportunity to paint a very real picture of what top-level athletes do, will continue to do, and won't do. The image of a top athlete that I paint for them runs counter to the Nike commercials, but mine is real. I use words like "disconnected," "alone," "sweaty." We've allowed our young athletes to be shaped by what they see and not what they need to do, so the first road block actually becomes what they know. My job is to kick them into what they don't know. I have to break their pattern.

I remember reading Mia Hamm's book when I was getting ready for high school soccer. The imagery was ignition for me: alone on the track, running until she puked. That's how she got there, so how would I be able to make it if I wasn't doing that? It sparked me to motion. As coaches and parents, our role is to do the same. To spark our young athletes into believing and working toward some level of personal betterment, even if that is difficult for both parties. "Whatever you've been doing, keep doing it," my high school coach said to me one day. Seven words were enough to indicate I was doing something right. That was all I needed. Just a little nudge. Keep going. Keep after it. Keep chasing. The power of positive feedback in this same narrative is critical. We love to chastise player mistakes and criticize decisions, but it's even more powerful and changing to uplift in one or two sentences.

Thus, our goal should be to support the conscious choices of young players to work hard, regardless of the outcome.

No athlete makes it to extreme levels without investing on their own—it's just not possible. Too many "talented" athletes who don't put in effort get washed out by decent athletes putting in effort. We need top athletes putting in major effort, so that the sport continues to get better. And honestly, at any level, why would you do anything if you're not going to put in effort? Had I just one dollar for every athlete who showed up and didn't put in effort, who thought showing up was enough, I'd be able to print this book on solid gold sheets. Showing up after we show up is mandatory for success in business, relationships, and sports.

Old school tactics sometimes can spur great responses from athletes. And I would encourage parents and coaches to consider them highly. I like to assign homework to my team as one way to structure outside work as a habit. Perhaps that's watching video on how to do a specific skill or letting them know that we'll have a juggling competition the following practice. This messaging needs to be echoed by everyone involved with a team or an athlete is doomed to mediocrity.

The mammoth hurdle to self-investment facing most athletes is lack of vision with regard to the benefit. When you work alone, you build something special within yourself. When it's not about someone else, when we can truly focus on our needs and weaknesses and hear our own thoughts as we go through it, something clicks into place. Training alone also has the differed benefit of understanding one's self, an important challenge in today's social atmosphere, and one certainly not discussed enough in the current educational climate. By encouraging and persuading my team to work on their own, I noticed that the girls had a better understanding of themselves. Suddenly, our talks were more open about strengths and weaknesses. Eventually, they begin to see that the path to self-awareness is a long and arduous one, and unless an athlete is willing to work on her own and work to understand her strengths and weaknesses, she is unlikely to move toward her best version of herself. Isn't that the ultimate goal for all of us overseeing young women?

Solo work in sports has other benefits. An astonishingly scary fact: a recent study showed that adult obesity rates are now higher than 35% in 9 states. It's above 25% in 47 states.[2] Sports are a great part of a healthy lifestyle, but only if fitness and workouts become part

---

[2] *"Obesity Rates: Adults." The State of Childhood Obesity,* **https://stateofchildhoodobesity.org/adult-obesity/**.

of your daily process. This has easily been the best asset I've taken from sports. I simply cannot go a long period of time without a serious workout.

By encouraging our youth to take part in their own fitness, we're unlocking them from the social stigma that comes with health. Further, without solo work, the team efforts are less rewarding. Psychologically, we all want to feel safe and surrounded by others we know respect us and take us seriously. Could sports, then, be one example of earning respect through work?

I challenge my team to grueling fitness drills, and I've received nothing but extremely positive feedback about that. One day in July my girls were training for high school tryouts on the local track when one of the boys' teams came in. We had already worked strenuously for 15 minutes. As I gave them a rest, they heard the boys' team complaining about lunges. I overheard these comments from my students:

> "I can't believe they're complaining about that."
>
> "I know, right? Coach works us ten times as hard."
>
> "Those boys wouldn't last a minute in our workout."

What was torture became pride.

Work Ethic

"When you are not practicing, someone else is.
When you meet [her], [she] will win."
Martial Arts Proverb

To play on my team, you must work. If you don't work hard, you'll either be cut or you'll sit. I'd take five players who work incredibly hard over 20 lazy-but-talented youngsters.

In 7th or 8th grade, players should start developing a better tactical understanding and should build new skillsets that come with better coordination. For some technical soccer terms, things like volleys, half-volleys, and combinations of touches, shields, passes, and turns become standard use as they progress, but the first time they try them, it generally looks like baby deer trying to rollerblade. You just don't know what you'll get. As you might expect, they get frustrated quickly. I can demo a volley well enough that it looks easy, but they struggle with it the first time they try it and say, "I'm not good at this." That is a dangerous phrase not to attack immediately.

I always respond the same way: "You're not good at it, *yet*. I've done this for many years now. Of course I'm better at it than you are on your first try." We accidently tend to communicate to athletes, especially to young women, that you're either good at something or you're not, which takes away all motivation to work at whatever that is. Add one word and the messaging completely changes. This is the fixed mindset rearing its ugly head again. I try to remind them that, at a certain point, they couldn't walk either. This is also a result of praising talented players over players who learn, grow, and adapt.

We have opportunities to drill into the minds of young athletes that they will need to practice something to become proficient. We miss them, frankly, favoring the short path over the real path. Once an athlete figures out this simple formula, the calculus becomes less enigmatic: Practice something, then get better, repeat the cycle, and impress a coach or other teammates, play more, do better, practice even more. It is vital to have rewards along the way, whether real or imagined. Otherwise, we won't know it's going well. This process, which includes the self-assessment I describe in Chapter 1, is the most effective means to success in any field, pursuit, or interest. Learning it in a sport translates directly to all areas of life.

There's science to back this emphasis on hard work. The term "muscle memory" floats around a lot, but the nerd in me wanted more. There is a compound found in the body called myelin. It's a layer that surrounds nerves like a casing. When you are moving, feeling, or sensing, nerves are firing signals from end to end across the axons (think of this as the wiring system) to the nerve cell body and onto the next set of axons. Myelin is the substance that keeps those signals moving efficiently and speedily. As you train, the fatty tissue sheath of myelin becomes attuned to what sequences need to happen. When you do something over and over, myelin builds up over the nerves you use, and the movement or activity becomes easier or requires less thought. Many think the science of this deeply explains athletic successes as well.[3]

In 2013, my team manager and the dad of one of my younger and, at the time, weaker players came to me at one of our team parties. He shared his gratitude for my relentless effort-focused badgering, sharing a story of his daughter's mathematical plight. "She came to me last night and asked for math help, but I wasn't able to do it, man! I thought, well, maybe I can get her a tutor, so I told her that I couldn't help and then I asked what she wanted to do." You may recall this story from earlier in the book, but her answer was so simple yet profound it bears repeating. He said, "Her response blew me away! She said, 'Don't worry, Daddy, I wasn't very good at left-footed passing, and I worked at it, and now I'm good. I'll just keep working on this and eventually, I'll be good at it.' "

He didn't need to say anything else.

In a survey when I asked what players wished their parents would have done, one player responded with "supported me first and foremost for having the opportunity to do something I love and not just for my successes on the field."

---

[3] *"How Myelination Can Make You a Better Athlete." Uphill Athlete, 3 April 2017,* **https://www.uphillathlete.com/myelination-make-you-better-athlete/**.

She wants this kind of support. Can we step up and deliver for her?

ACTION STEPS FOR THIS CHAPTER

Create these with your family:

- Have an open discussion about your daughter's goals. Ask many questions, assert very little. By asking questions, like "How do you think you can get there?" you can help her find the steps to get there and the initiative will come from her. Her ideas are powerful!

- What can you do to support your young athlete doing some work on her own for just 10 minutes a day? Can you create a break time? Help her get started? Does she need equipment? Is there a place you can go with her?

- What are some rewards for hard work that you can create together? Are there ways to support her working independently that don't place an emphasis on the outcome? Can you reward her for time invested in the craft instead of the number of points she scores? Can you reward her for practice outside of practice?

CHAPTER 5

Injury and Failure: Both Should Be Parts of Her Life

"When you take risks, you learn that there will be times when you succeed, and there will be times when you fail, and both are equally important."

Ellen DeGeneres

Ellen Sandseter wrote a theoretical article on children's risky play from an evolutionary perspective. She postulates that six distinct activities and experiences are key to the development of coping skills, which help people master both situations and stimuli they had previously feared. She takes an approach I admire: distinguishing between hazards as a negative component and risks as a positive component and building a child's risk management and perception skills.

Children's Risky Play from an Evolutionary Perspective

Categories and subcategories of risky play
(revised from Sandseter, 2007a, 2007b)

CATEGORIES	RISK	SUBCATEGORY
Great heights	Danger of injury from falling	Climbing Jumping from still or flexible surfaces Balancing on high objects Hanging/swinging at great heights
High speed	Uncontrolled speed and pace that can lead to collision with something (or someone)	Swinging at high speed Sliding and sledging at high speed Running uncontrollably at high speed Bicycling at high speed Skating and skiing at high speed
Dangerous tools	Can lead to injuries and wounds	Cutting tools: Knives, saws, axes Strangling tools: Ropes, etc.
Dangerous elements	Where children can fall into or from something	Cliffs Deep water or icy water Fire pits
Rough-and-tumble	Where the children can harm each other	Wrestling Fencing with sticks, etc. Play fighting
Disappear/get lost	Where the children can disappear from the supervision of adults, get lost alone	Go exploring alone Playing alone in unfamiliar environments

Often, we associate risk with danger and, ultimately, we avoid it completely. If we can address those fears, we can teach daughters to address them and find that instead of a fear, a risk of failure or failure itself can be the most important lesson of all.

Failure is a word that seems to be offensive in today's times, but an athlete is only as strong as the hell she goes through. Significant avoidance of failure is what I like to refer to as "the bubble," and it's where many of my friends live. Safe. Secure. Serene. Life's great in the bubble. You never get hurt, you can't fail, and you won't stumble. You never get hurt because the bubble (someone else, privilege, income, race) shields you. You can't fail because you won't be allowed to. The bubble will insulate you from risk, and you won't stumble because the floor underneath you is made of marble, so there are no sharp edges or holes.

Those friends of mine got crushed when they got to the real world. We don't keep in touch much—for good reason, too. They aren't happy. They aren't taking after their dreams, and they aren't willing to work hard enough and push through failure to reach the best version of themselves. They won't make change, and therefore, can't grow. They can't have tough conversations, so they avoid relationships that challenge them. They devolve.

The assumption they made of the world was based on a red carpet mentality instilled by their parents. Didn't make the team? Mom will fix it. Didn't get into the program you wanted? Dad will call and sort it out. Didn't get accepted to your first-choice college? Don't worry! We'll just call and raise hell until we get you what you want (or what you think she wants).

Failure isn't a bad thing, and neither is pain. As adults, we get kicked when we're down, go through hard times, battle depression, and fight through loss of loved ones. As I write this, my dad is in the hospital, my grandmother passed on three weeks ago, and we lost my family dog a few weeks before that. You can't shield someone from that!!

Failure is a part of our existence. It's the gray area that embodies both the good and the bad. As we monitor and interact with young women who are playing a sport, we've got to keep careful watch on how much insulation we're providing. Some is fine, but protection from the reality of sports (more on that in the next chapter) and the difficulty you might go through to find even moderate success is fundamentally damaging to your daughter's ability to cope with real life outside the bubble: careers, work, bosses, and all the rest of the stuff we deal with out here. Mistakes and failures are real. We leaders must stop giving her the pretense that bad things are never going to happen.

On the bright side, there's little to compare success to without the comparison to failure. If you diminish the value of failure, what then should we offer our kids in contrast? I detest participation trophies. For the same reason that failure is important, participation shouldn't be rewarded. There are few circumstances as an adult where I receive any recognition for simply showing up, and I don't believe that to be a valuable lesson for our youth. I do see many failures, almost daily, and without an understanding of what failure represents and how to cope with it, I would be rendered immobile.

Participation in sports can single-handedly build coping mechanisms.

Failure is a noun, but it should always apply to an experience, not a person. Never under any circumstance should a young woman be called a failure. They are NOT failures, no matter how much difficulty they are facing or how unsuccessful any attempt may be. Instead, use the verb "fail." It can be an action, and therefore is something they do, did, or have done. In this manner, it can be referred to as an action that requires further analysis, a new plan, and a new effort. Our students are not failures, and as a coach, parent, or caregiver, your words have the power to create a self-image. *Be mindful of your terms.* Language is all we have to make distinctions between concepts that can be either uplifting or damaging.

A player fails. A team fails. We fail. There was a failure. That was a failure.

Never: You are a failure.

As a method of approach to sports and to other things as well, failure should be encouraged. In fact, in youth players, those who are able to fail more will undoubtedly perform better. As a construct, we are encouraging the development of a working, analytical mind, fostered in an environment that requires that type of thinking. That environment is created by you in several ways. Risk is an important part of life. Why not engage with it early, understand it, and be given the space to enjoy it? That's my hope for the daughters of all of my readers, now and in the future.

This is also where most parents lose. If you want your daughter to develop, the buzzword of the decade in sports, but you don't want her to fail, you are in *violation* of her growth.

Failure and growth do not exist outside of one another.

Failure and Praise

The most important aspect of failure calibration is praise. If you whisk an attempt with the right ingredients, the failure becomes a more saturated learning experience. Praise is that engine. The more consistently you can praise your daughters' attempts at things they had not previously attempted, the easier the analysis will be following the attempt. Let them try. Laugh with them, coach them, ask them about it. And then let them at it again and again. The only thing that should stop the cycle is her choice to avoid it. If they only did things that worked out the first time they tried them, you'd not only have a team with stagnant skills, you'd rob your daughters of the opportunities for personal growth. You'd have a luck-of-the-draw system, where skills became imprinted only if they worked. It would put incredible pressure on you as a coach. Instead of sharing a skill and letting them try it, you'd have to rehearse the mechanics, review the concepts, and then prepare them mentally for the testing phase and then give them one shot at it and judge them on the result.

Where else is this messed up practice? Oh, yes. Education. Schooling is based on this exact principle. I'm working on that with Ortus Academy—but that's another whole book project!

Encouraging your daughter to understand that something failed, then to build an environment that supports her exploration of it is paramount, and it happens through appropriately applied praise. Open ended questions are simple and effective ways to create this environment. "Why didn't that work?" or "What would you do differently?" become support networks for a failed attempt to climb to a successful endeavor. Practice praising the effort instead of the talent, as it is certainly more responsible for success than talent. For every five athletes competing at a high level, another 30 who possessed the equivalent raw talent did not put in the effort to stay on top of their game and did not achieve as much as the player who worked hard and who learned from failure.

As you praise the young women in your world, remember to level your tone and focus on the behavior that you want more than what you don't. Contrast is an effective tool: *Don't do this, do this.* Without both, your message isn't as easily absorbed. The contrast you use is still only as effective as your tone and your words.

It is not our successes that define us, but how we deal with failure, and as the role model, you're going to define their dealings with failure. Be mindful of your response.

Injuries Are Important

"It's always hard to deal with injuries mentally, but I like to think about it as a new beginning. I can't change what happened, so the focus needs to go toward healing and coming back stronger than before."

Carli Lloyd

I might sound radical suggesting that injuries are an important part of a player's psyche, but this flows from a good place. I promise.

Imagine getting all A's all your life without ever trying. Then out of nowhere—BOOM: your first D. You probably wouldn't even know how to respond or react. You'd start breathing heavily, sweating profusely, and getting fidgety. That panic might take you weeks to overcome, only after you're ready to admit, own it, and talk about it.

Then you move on. You analyze the circumstances and details. You make a list of changes you'll implement, and you return to the drawing board. It's not about getting a poor grade. It's about learning to deal with it appropriately and successfully.

Some players naturally deal with injury better. Maybe they are more levelheaded, maybe they have dealt with them previously and understand the process. But most are lacking the ability to handle the process of an injury because they've never had it expressed to them. If you can help them see the end, and paint the vision of a return to the sport after checking off this list, you may help them deal with it appropriately and successfully .

However, the feelings associated with injury can vary, namely because injuries vary. Not only do injuries have individual severity associated with them, but the duration of recovery time needed, the reaction to news, and the way it was delivered can also vary greatly.

Still, it's important to understand that injuries are a part of the game as is the process by which we recover from them.

Injury Phases (in layman's terms):

Injury
Assessment/Diagnoses
Rehabilitation/Recovery
Return

If you need to find more resources, you can certainly investigate the Phases of Rehabilitation online. There is a wide array of different opinions, assessment parameters, and quantities of phases, but most all contain some of the same variables. My goal here is not to inform you of the science in a field where I have zero training but to point to the overarching experience that your player will ultimately face, even if that experience is a short, narrow, and docile one.

One of my players has dealt with injury fairly consistently, so it doesn't affect her as it might with some others. She wasn't emotional. She knows the toll that injuries take on the regular practice schedule, but clearly also can embody what it means to take the slow road of recovery. I'm proud of her, but not because I did anything special to assist her.

Did you know that ACL injuries are more common in women?

In a man's hips, a straight line runs from hip to knee to foot. In women, who have larger hips, that line from hip to knee to ankle changes, widening as girls get older. If they experience massive forces from ankle up to the hips, which can come from running, jumping and landing, or turning, the force isn't straight. The shearing that occurs when forces designed to be straight are a little off center causes things like tendons and ligaments to stress. When those stresses maximize, things pop. In ligaments, where motion is meant to be in linear directions, that off-center force coming from wider hips has massive magnitude, resulting in more common ACL tears. This is key in any sport.

A tear doesn't have to be the end of an athletic career though. Many players make full recoveries. How much would you like to bet that most of those returning athletes understand what it will take to recover from injury? It's important that you as coach or some other mentor have the right discussions with your player if she's injured. If you haven't gone through a serious injury yourself, find someone who has and have them speak to her.

Talking with an injured player can be tricky and feel

very complicated. We know it's not the end of the world, but it could become the end of her world if she doesn't have the right vantage point (or, even worse, if you don't have the right vantage point and you brand her to think the same as you). Some players see injury as the end of their career. Some see it as the end of the world. Some see it as a hurdle. Regardless, a discussion that takes place about injury should be centered around listening for understanding before shifting into insights, advice, and instruction.

Players with injuries face two major battles: Will I be able to play again? And will this injury be a limiting factor moving forward? Even if they make it past the first hurdle, the second is just as daunting. I was told by several doctors I'd never play soccer again after tearing my right quadriceps (right thigh muscle) in my senior year of high school. Yet, I put in the work to make a full recovery and played in college. Screw you, doctors! The body is way more adaptable than we give it credit for being. Injuries are a part of the sport. They're common. And if we, as the caregivers and role models, are incredibly powerful at manipulating younger perspectives, the lurking question is will we use this power to help them see a future *beyond* an injury instead of a future *because* of an injury.

Mind the way you talk to your young woman about her injury. Love her when she needs it and give her the support she craves when she asks for it. Both will help her heal faster (mentally). I don't have the degree or the education to talk about what the body can and can't do, but I can attest to seeing and being close to many different triumphs over cancers, accidents, amputations, and birth defects that have left people WAY worse off than the injuries most athletes will struggle with. Managing the journey of an injury (the pain, the recovery, the energy, the mental battle) is an important one for every athlete to become familiar with.

Even if the injury is minor, having an understanding of our coping ability and the need for mental support and fortitude can be worth its weight in long-term gold.

Overall, the ability for players to manage and navigate the waters of an injury are a better indicator, in my experience, for how far a player's career can go and how well they can manage what's necessary to succeed. That success could come on or off the field, so I'm particularly mindful not to create fear around the word "injury" on my teams and in my circle.

My players have dealt with injury in a variety of ways, but they learn to see it as another challenge to overcome.

CHAPTER 6

The Sheer Math of Youth Sports

"Find your self-respect now.
Don't dumb yourselves down. Think of yourself as capable and worthy of finding a guy who is going to respect you, too. It's so important, I mean, and the confidence you get from feeling smart and tackling something like mathematics, which is a challenge, right? Math is hard."

Danica McKellar

There are two options in sports as I see it. You either work really hard and take all of your sport experiences into a professional career or you learn a lot about life, success, teamwork, yourself, and you conquer other mountains that make you happy.

Your Data Is Stupid

A parent told me her 10-year-old daughter was on the second-highest ranked team in the state. I think she expected me to somehow widen my gaze and bestow on her the parent-of-the-year award for birthing a soccer stud.

This ranking system has taken over. Days, sometimes weeks before games, parents will enlighten me with data about the team we're playing, the tournament we're in, and the current points needed to take us to the next rank. I get it—you're invested.

But as a coach, this is not only data that isn't helpful, it's actually harmful to team development.

The points are arbitrary. The ranking is arbitrary. The value we place on it, both arbitrary and misplaced.

What would you feel if someone, say an older suitor for your daughter, walked by and ranked her? They assigned her a number and determined that's her value.

How would that make you feel?

My point is simple: No one gives a damn about rankings except you and the other families on the team *at best*.

The way in which we use these points to start team drama, provoke other families, create jealousy from other teams, and evaluate the team's value is worth reevaluating. If your daughter has a bad game, making light of a drop in rank should take little priority over being a supportive parent for her. But I've seen so many conversations break hearts because they stem from parental ego management issues, all circling from ranking systems that really have no place at the table.

This goes double if your child is younger than 13.

Rankings shouldn't be calculated until high school, when we uncuff players from solely developing and let them really focus on the results. Better said, *caring* about the ranking is the issue, not the ranking itself. It doesn't have merit or value unless we give it value. Alone, it's worth about as much as a cup of yellow snow.

Other data has about the same value.

Parents: There's one move you can always count on to drastically reduce your daughter's likelihood of being on my team or that of any coach who's really good at developing players and creating a positive team culture. It's to say something like, "On her last team she averaged 1.2 goals per game and was the second highest assist leader."

What's your objective here?

Instead of sending an endearing message about how much you want your daughter to grow, get better, enjoy the game, and learn to compete at a high level (all her choices), you've planted your ego as the center of attention between me and giving her a fair chance at growing under my instruction.

Those stats tell me nothing about where she is developmentally. Is this a JV team at your elite private school? Is it just a rec league team made up of community members who simply get together Saturday mornings to kick the ball around? Even if it's a club team, a step up from rec, I still don't know anything about her skills. Your comment gives me no context about what type of player or teammate she is.

The stats you hold in such high regard don't tell me what kind of work ethic she has. And by shoving the data in front of me like an overbearing waiter at a restaurant, I can only draw one conclusion: You're *THAT* type of parent, the kind who potentially tracks stats at a soccer game for 10 year olds, screams orders from the sidelines, or worst, berates your kid for low numbers in the car. You're possibly damaging her confidence by using numbers to make comparisons. And, worst of all, you risk damaging her feelings of self-worth by applying a numeric system to a childhood pastime.

Why are we creating data for kids and presenting them as assessment of value? If the data is ever important to a coach and to a player, it comes from only two places:

The team is tracking every element of data (not just things like goals, but things like passing accuracy, etc.) and they are presented as a means for the team to improve overall scores. Again, measurement is fine, but the context is important.

Within the team's individual stakeholders, if data is to be used, it needs to be used unilaterally. Each position may have a different metric (goals scored for forwards and goals conceded for keepers, perhaps), with the objective being to give each player a measurable element to work to improve. It makes no fair sense to use goals scored to compare players in defensive positions.

If you are out there tracking your daughter's scoring, assists, steals, three-pointers, etc. (whatever sport, whatever time), why are you doing it? Is it to fuel your ego and give an edge to any comparisons you make of her to other players?

Is it to strengthen your position that she is the best at a certain part of the game? Cut those objectives completely from your world.

You have other things to focus on, such as enjoying the marvel of watching your child work and enjoying a game. The most important things she wants from you are love and psychological safety. Throwing out numbers as a comparison is a great way to indicate you don't actually care about her, just the score. That's what coaches care about, and that's a critical distinction.

The Numbers of Future Lies We Tell

Looking at sports as a mathematical equation helps me identify why I coach as fervently as I do. Soccer has given me everything, so I think it's important that coaches and parents recognize what it can and cannot be about for most players and understand that they themselves can drive impact on a deeper level by understanding these engines.

When I first entered the job scene out of college, I remember feeling like the world was weightless. I was dominant at everything that I attempted, or so I felt. But that wasn't always the case, and later in life, I was challenged more and had to do more. Weight eventually hit me. It always does.

I was ready though because through sports I learned enough about myself to propel me through the tough times. I knew where I was strong and where I was weak—a calculation that isn't necessarily broached in standard education. I understood the discipline and rigorous work that it took to get better at something, and I had learned to deal with failure, whether that be injury or other emotional setbacks. I deciphered the puzzle behind setting a goal and hitting it, knowing that it would not come without investment, and I figured out how to motivate myself, even when I had doubts. Essentially, I had been given the opportunity to experience in a healthy way measurement, failure, injury, open-ended conversations from parents, good and bad team environments, regular solitude, and strong work ethic. So why then, is it important to understand the math?

In our day and age, the allure of professional sports exists in two distinct categories across any sport: prestige and salary.

Many players play the game because they love it. They love the sweat, the work, the pain, the competition, and the rewards. We grow up watching an arena full of lights with talented players accomplishing magical athletic feats, and it inspires us to grasp for greatness. We're painfully aware of the earning potential of professional athletes, of course. While the minimum salary in the NWSL is not necessarily the most attractive figure, it has increased significantly over the last decade and is expected to inflate to rival other professional sports. I certainly believe it should. More importantly, the financial lure does have a significant coupling effect with a love for the game. Still, we must understand that the level of play that we see and how easy professional athletes make it look are quite contrary to the reality. It's hard as hell to get there. Until we accept that, these numbers just seem like numbers. We must ask the question, what story do the numbers tell us?

Let's take a look at some numbers released by the NCAA. This chart shows the numbers of players who played in high school and those who went on to play in college.

NCAA

ESTIMATED PROBABILITY OF COMPETING IN COLLEGE ATHLETICS

Women	HIGH SCHOOL PARTICIPANTS	NCAA PARTICIPANTS	OVERALL % HS TO NCAA	% HS TO NCAA DIVISION I	% HS TO NCAA DIVISION II	% HS TO NCAA DIVISION III
Basketball	430,368	16,532	3.8%	1.2%	1.1%	1.5%
Cross Country	226,039	15,966	7.1%	2.6%	1.8%	2.7%
Field Hockey	60,549	6,066	10.0%	3.0%	1.3%	5.7%
Golf	75,605	5,372	7.1%	2.9%	2.1%	2.2%
Ice Hockey	9,599	2,355	24.5%	8.8%	1.2%	14.5%
Lacrosse	93,473	11,752	12.6%	3.7%	2.7%	6.2%
Soccer	388,339	27,638	7.1%	2.4%	1.9%	2.8%
Softball	367,405	19,999	5.4%	1.7%	1.6%	2.1%
Swimming	170,797	12,684	7.4%	3.3%	1.2%	2.9%
Tennis	187,519	8,736	4.7%	1.5%	1.1%	2.1%
Track & Field	494,477	29,907	6.0%	2.7%	1.5%	1.8%
Volleyball	444,779	17,387	3.9%	1.2%	1.1%	1.6%
Water Polo	20,826	1,159	5.6%	3.4%	0.9%	1.3%

SOURCES: High school figures from the 2016-17 High School Athletics Participation Survey conducted by the National Federation of State High School Associations; data from club teams not included. College numbers from the NCAA 2016-17 Sports Sponsorship and Participation Rates Report. **(Last updated: April 20, 2018)**

I'm not at all surprised by these numbers, but maybe you are. I've carried three teams of players to the age where college selection was an option. While I'm not typically coaching a top-tier team, I still have players who could consider collegiate sports. Very few high school players end up on a college team, so that shouldn't be the goal. If it is the objective for you as a parent, perhaps your daughter should consider ice hockey where the percentages are greater.

More troublesome than the erroneous assumption that high school play will create a pipeline to college play is the perspective parents have which creates unachievable expectations. Here are three of my least-favorite but top quotes about college sports:

- "My daughter's going to get a scholarship."
- "She loves playing soccer. I can't imagine her not playing in college."
- "We keep telling her if she wants to play at (insert college name), she'll have to get a scholarship."

Have you ever said something like this?

Here's a direct quote from a player of mine when I asked how parents could be better for their soccer experience:

> *"I think in general parents of female athletes need to better understand the world of college recruiting and the toll it takes on their children. I found*

> *the entire process so stressful and was under constant pressure from my parents to send emails to coaches and research college programs. In the end, it played a role in my decision not to continue to be recruited. I believe parents of female athletes are the main cause of all the "craziness" of recruiting, specifically because of the draw of athletic scholarships and the prestige that a spot on a D1 team can get you. I wish the whole recruiting process didn't make my parents lose sight of the fact that I play soccer because I love the game."*

Here, parents are assuming soccer is a payday loan for education and that our current 14-year-old will want to continue playing forever. I've had players tell me on a Tuesday, after a great practice on Monday, that they don't want to play soccer anymore. I've also had players tell me, away from parents, that they play just to make Mom or Dad happy. There are degrees of truth in these stories, of course, but there is a point that is still incredibly valid and important for us. It is critical to learn and understand what players actually want, making sure that it is indeed what they want for themselves while ensuring that we are not trying to push them into a paycheck (scholarship). I've seen so many parents sending kids to private trainers for session after session, not so the kids can get better and develop but so they can earn a scholarship.

Many college players admit that the sport feels like a job, and they walk from the noisy push we as coaches and parents place on them. I've done it wrong sometimes. I'm writing this out of my mistakes too, remember!

The important driver for any player who ascends to the next level of play after youth sports is a simple one. The drive is perpetual growth. Think of Carli Lloyd, Mia Hamm, Jackie Joyner-Kersee. Try to find me a famous female athlete and tell me they didn't consistently improve from the age of 10, and tell me they did it for someone else. It has to come from them! So if you hear your kid commenting on how she enjoys other things or wants to be a professional artist, *listen*. The crucial part of listening is letting her speak for herself. We may make assumptions about the girls and what they need. I do, even as just a coach, so I can only imagine what it's like with more investment. I'm sure it's hard. I know it is. I still have to catch myself realizing and being self-aware enough to stop.

As the influential adults in her world, we must examine our motivations for her success in the first place. Are you saddled with emotional baggage from a time you were cut from your high school team? Are you out to prove your athletic lineage through your daughter? Are you irrationally emotional because she didn't pick the career you'd have chosen for her? Were you dreaming of college sports, and are you excited to live your dreams vicariously through your offspring? Reduce your baggage to a carry-on, please.

She's capable of her own magic and accomplishment. She doesn't exist to fulfill your dreams and achieve your goals. Your dream should be to uplift her to her own idea of success, and these numbers, and the story behind them, may help you realize how important it is for her to choose this sport for herself before she submits to all she will need to take on to make it.

Collegiate sports require sacrifice, hardship, and talent. Many players get there and don't like it. Some get there and love it. Can you guess which ones continue to grow? Numbers and percentages are not a reason to crush someone's dream. Hell, I played Division I college soccer and I walked-on. Oddity? Check. But that was because I deeply loved it, wanted it, and when it came to my parents, I don't remember a single time where they pushed me to or from soccer. They just let it be my relationship to the game. And I'm grateful for that, and I want that for all of my players and for yours too.

The Data Suggests that the End Game Could Be Learning the Process

Not many players move on after high school to play at the next level. We've got that. But if we *accept* that, we get to revel in the exquisite marvels that come from developing a mindset, skillset, set of habits, and work ethic through sport. We can truly appreciate it, forget the score, and love the game. Scores count, measurement is important, but remember, we're not her fans touting records and planning parades. We're the wind beneath her wings.

The NCAA did not publish data related to NCAA women who successfully transitioned to professional play, but that seems understandable given the massive scale of women's collegiate soccer and the miniscule scale of professional women's soccer. Hopefully the two balance more evenly in the near future, especially after a solid World Cup performance in the summer of 2015, a world cup title in 2019, a feature in TIME magazine of the US Women's National Team, and more notoriety of women in sports like soccer.

But for argument's sake, let's use the Men's numbers. Of 417,419 high school players, 5.7% played in college, meaning that of 400,000, only 23,792 played in any college atmosphere. Of those almost 24,000 players, 1.4% went professional, leaving us with a total of 333 athletes who transitioned: 333/417,419 = .000797. There is about a 7% chance that your kid has a 1% chance to play professionally, or, if you like numbers and zeros, a .07% chance.

I don't like thinking of players and people this way. As an entrepreneur, I have to believe I'll win, even if the odds aren't in my favor. But I need to know the odds. And, I need to be willing to do what it takes to be a part of that upper percentage.

Now, a dream is not a statistic to your kid. Your kid is a living breathing athlete, so this isn't just a stat that illustrates their chances. They can influence this number. The number simply tells us there are hundreds of thousands of people competing for only hundreds of spaces. Even within this reality of numerical representation is the truth that having a sport, something you LOVE, become a job can be different. This does matter. It means not only do we have to be talented to get there, but we must also bring something more to the table. In general, those aren't betting odds. Those players who do beat these odds are STILL often left in a position to re-evaluate their careers after just a short stint within the field. The body cannot sustain such intense physical demands for a long period of time, and some athletes quickly lose love for the game when political agendas, money, and a year packed full of red-eye flights, hotels, and meals-on-the-go are finally in hand.

Statistically speaking, the average playing career for an NFL player is 3.5 years, the average MLB career is 5.6 years, the average NBA career is 4.8 years, and the average NHL career is 5.5 years. No matter what her sport is, we as caregivers are there to be supportive, even if it's not a long career.

If it's true that sports don't offer long career possibilities, then it behooves players, even players who do make it to professional levels, to learn valuable takeaways from the game in their youth, because most of them end up playing for fun afterwards, coaching, investing, or otherwise at some point. In my experience, there are only two ways that a young adult, no matter how astute, will develop a taste for the lessons that come from sports:

1. *They are told that they are part of a lesson. They experience the lesson. They surpass an obstacle related to the lesson, and the lesson then shows them the benefit therein.*

2. *They become wiser with age and start to see connection between sports and other aspects of life and bridge the two.*

The former is a coaching responsibility, but it is also one that you can help reinforce at home. It's not hard either. It's a coach's duty not only to guide them through the lessons that will drive long-term impact but to make it clear to them what they are going to take away and why. They may not hear you the first time, but as you go through the process, you'll drive impact at a much faster rate, effectively multiplying the benefit the youth receive.

It's the WHY that good coaches share. You can support that too.

In 2013, I met a young lady named Anna. Anna was technically unsound, physically capable, but emotionally disconnected from the game. The coach prior to me had eroded the confidence that she possessed, so she feared me prior to my start, expecting my approach to match that of her former coach. I'm a firm believer that there are ways to coach women without, at any given point, directly telling a player that she's a bad player. There are more words in the English language than most people can count, so for Anna to have heard things like "you're a trash player" or "you're not good at soccer" is part of my reason for writing this book.

No one should ever hear those words from a coach or leader.

I took Anna aside one day during one-on-ones and asked her to perform a stepover to beat a defender to the left. After it was successful, she looked back at me and smiled brightly. I saw then that it wasn't her skill that needed development; it was her confidence. I immediately flooded her with both positive and constructive feedback. It would take lots of feedback to build her skills where she could feel as though what was working was noticed and what wasn't working was corrected.

In five weeks Anna had developed enough to earn more and more playing time, and her confidence grew. The more you put in, the more you get out, I would tell her. I was consistent with the team, not just her, about that, and as time went on and Anna got better and better, other players started to notice and mimic the amount of extra, outside-of-practice labor Anna was putting in.

After the season, Anna wrote about what she had learned through the year.

> *I believe that sports teach you more than how to kick a ball, or how to hit a birdie, or how to throw and catch. I believe that through sports, I learn lessons that will stick with me for the rest of my life. I believe these lessons are ones that will carry me through joy and sadness, through job interviews and layoffs, and ultimately carry me through life.*
>
> *Last year, I started playing club soccer. I had played rec for six years but had never been that serious about it. So when I entered the more competitive world of soccer, I probably looked like a deer in the headlights. I had never been the fastest one to run a mile. I had never been the one to play*

four different sports, all equally well. But I had made a commitment to something I wanted to do, and nothing could stop me from trying my best. Or so I thought. Then came long fitness practices that tested my will and my strength. I wanted to give up. But I didn't. I learned to persevere. I convinced myself that every sprint, every sit-up, every hurdle that I did would be one closer to being a good soccer player. I convinced myself that if I ran harder than everyone else, I would be closer to being a star player. And so I pushed myself, and still do.

Another lesson came through the championship game of a tournament. It was tied 0-0 with only five minutes left. The other team came rushing down the field. Our defense tried to stop them. And what did the ref do? He blew his whistle. A handball in the box. There had never been a handball. And as soon as he blew the whistle, the dynamic of the game changed. It felt like they had already scored, that the game was already over. I wanted to protest. I wanted to punch the ref in the face. But I didn't. Because I learned to hold my tongue.

I remind myself of these lessons all the time. My thoughts of wanting to give up or fight back haven't changed, but my reaction to it has. Now, it makes me try harder. If a ref gives another team a goal, it doesn't feel as though I've lost, it feels as though I haven't tried as hard as I could have. And that just fuels the fire inside of me that wants to win, that wants success.

> *I haven't become that star player that I want to be, and maybe I never will. But to me, what counts is that I'm trying. And even if I don't keep playing, I will look back on it and see soccer as more than a sport. I'll see the friendships I made and the joy that it has brought me. And I'll remind myself of these lessons as they carry me through life.*

By consistently reinforcing the relationship between hard work and results, I was forging a connection that would only develop faster. I expect that every person who plays competitive sports will eventually see the correlation. However, I expect when they are exposed to the correlation and then allowed to explore it, the reality to a person becomes permanent, and they can connect that correlated work-to-outcome connection to things like school, careers, and relationships. Can we be the ones who help them make these connections faster, stronger, and at a more meaningful rate?

A girl who understands that hard work begets results will certainly go farther than one who simply plays the game. More importantly, a girl who learns these lessons early can drive herself farther than someone simply listening and repeating. Moreover, an athlete who has found success and now represents herself differently, in the realm of business for example, knows and understands the engine from which skill is born instead of looking at a foreign trait and assuming it came naturally or was given to a person externally. She will understand that it is a consistent effort and persevering mind that will find success in any field, and that lesson is most important to a young woman.

Anna was one of my more consistent players. She's always very energized, and now knows that she can accomplish anything she wants to because of her work ethic. She's battled injuries and minor setbacks, but still understands that the difference between those that do and those that do not *is her*.

Data That Isn't Stupid

Telling someone that there is a 1% chance they will play pro is fine if you provide the context of how that relates to working harder than 99% of people. That's one way to do it. A way not to do it is to use numbers to suggest that only 1% of players make it and leave it at that. I know 80% of businesses fail within a five-year period. That's data. But when I think about it, and what I know to be true, is that 20% succeed. That context is all I need to continue to contribute to the craft I love.

The future is unknown for all of us. Data can be damaging or uplifting, and we are the ones able to influence with it. Your daughter is capable of amazing things, odds against her or not. Your daughter is also capable of switching attention and finding passion in other things. We exist in the betterment of her and her dreams, not to selfishly adhere to some kind of arranged-marriage end goal. The faster we realize our best outcome is her best opportunity, the more effectively we can breathe into her the gift that is true support.

I've learned a lot of lessons in the practice of pitching my business.

I've been told it will never work and that no one would pay for what we made. But people have.

I've been told we'd never raise capital. But we did.

I've been told we'd never become profitable. We haven't—not yet.

Those pieces of data matter, but it's my decision to head that direction anyway. So the data isn't right or wrong, it's just a way for us to create context.

As you go about the remainder of this book, remember that this chapter isn't about scaring your daughter away from her dream. Instead, it's about helping her realize what the cost of the dream is.

What I see more commonly than anything, which culminates from the past 5 chapters, is entitlement. Because parents are unwilling to let their daughter experience pain, measurement, failure, reality, daughters end up thinking no matter what they want, they can and should have it.

I believe the world to be a warm, inviting, welcoming place to those who navigate their relationships with kindness and gratitude. Still, it's not unkind to be real. Many athletes want to be the 1%, traveling and playing their sport for a living, making 6-figure salaries, and wearing the newest equipment on covers of magazines and ads.

This is a perfectly fine dream, if you're willing to give

top 1% kind of effort. If you're unwilling to work harder than 99% of people, then I don't believe you deserve to get something that 99% of people never will.

To me it's a simple calculus. It's not a secret, and the data supports that this math is still upheld in athletics.

We witnessed the passing of basketball legend Kobe Bryant. He wasn't a legend because he was good enough. He was a legend because he got up at 4:00 a.m. and worked out 4-6 hours a day when rookies put in 30 minutes. His 6-10x effort is what made him a legend.

What kind of effort is your daughter willing to give? And more importantly, how can we support maximum effort if she is serious about sports at the next level?

Finally, if she's not about sports at the next level, can we let go of the needs of our ego to let her gather lessons from the sport that are worth hundreds of thousands of future decision-making dollars?

ACTION ITEMS FOR THIS CHAPTER

If you're going to talk to your daughter about soccer at the next level because that's her dream, ask questions like:

- If data suggests that less than 1% of players make it to that level, what does working on your craft regularly mean for your chances?

- How can I support you getting there?
- What kind of environment do you need to be able to reach these goals?
- How long do you have before you need to be ready, and what kind of plan is needed to make sure you're ready on time?

If you're going to talk to your daughter about sports but she doesn't want to play at the next level, try these:

- What parts of [the sport] can you apply to school or relationships or real life?
- How does sports relate to success in careers?
- How can I support you having a great sport experience without you feeling like I'm pushing you any particular direction?
- What do you need to have a great [sport] experience this year?

CHAPTER 7

Winning Isn't Really about You

"Instead of letting your hardships and failures discourage or exhaust you, let them inspire you. Let them make you even hungrier to succeed."

Michelle Obama

As we stated from the beginning, this book is about showcasing the constructs of human relationships that allow for the most fluid and natural talent-expansion and identifying some of the nefarious enemies of rapid growth.

Most often, we place obstacles in the way of our athletes. We chastise them in the car, we fail to let them fail and learn, and we don't hold the process as queen. But now we're talking about something even deeper. Now we're talking about you.

I don't know you yet. I'd like to. You can find me on social media (Instagram @AaronVelky, or on Facebook: Aaron Velky), comment on the book's Facebook page, search for the "Let Her Play Community" or send me an email. All of that is public because I'm not afraid of hearing from you. I hope this book helps many parents develop the perspective that lets their daughter grow. I don't know you, but I know you're valuable. I know you have a beating heart and things to offer the world. I know you have an amazing daughter, one who surely loves you. I know moms overcome something as painful as childbirth to bring to this world a new light, and I know we've all overcome countless challenges that we'd never want to relive. That's what makes you strong. That's something I see even without seeing you. If I can see that through the outstretched arms of this book as you turn page to page, then I believe I can also help you see that same strength that you passed on to your daughter.

And yet, you may be one of many parents who evaluate your parenting according to whether or not your daughter wins. That notion is contradictory to all the growth potential we've just explored together, and it will quickly eliminate the self-confidence and worth of your daughter if you're not careful.

Let's make a few things clear:

1. *I'm writing to parents, caregivers. Players should want to win with a fervent hunger like a wolf in the winter cold. But this is about you—so I'm writing about your perspective.*

2. *You may have to stop and pause and reflect before you know whether or not you are guilty of any behaviors that are present in previous or coming examples. The tendency is to say, "That parent is CRAZY." Transparently, 80% of the people who comment on how crazy soccer parents are exhibit those same behaviors. Introspection lies ahead.*

3. *Whether your daughter is on a nationally ranked team and on track to play in college or playing high level ball with zero desire to play at the next level is irrelevant. The players I've seen overcome everything need an environment that embodies this chapter's root lesson.*

Most of us think of winning as a product. Something that you produce through your workouts, trainings, shoe color, height, performance. To me winning is just a green light on the avenue of sports growth. To me, the product, the thing I want my students to take away, is the process. The process is never-ending. You train, you work, you improve, you fail, you work , you grow, you try, you succeed, you work, you improve . . . it doesn't end. As a byproduct of this process, you earn your wins.

To build successful teams, we coaches need buy-in. If we get just 1% better each day, by the end of the regular season, we'd be 72% better than we started, which is massive. Maybe not enough to take a title, but growth. Players have to buy into the process. This process is important to understand. When we win, it signals that we're on the right path, are growing, and are improving.

When we lose, it indicates we have weaknesses, and we have things to work on still. **I want parents, players, and coaches to know what happens when we win and what is different if we lose, and how to keep our perspective on the prize.** At the adolescent age, that's what I care about. Improving. When you're into late high school, it's about results, but we supporters of daughters need to understand this relationship of wins and losses so we can be the support. Otherwise, we just contribute to the chaos.

Growth Mentality

We win because we've grown enough; we lose because we haven't. And therein lies the special ingredient of youth sports: growing. Given that most sports are team sports, you have to take into account that one player is statistically unlikely to render any result alone. In soccer, a dominant forward can't win a game alone without preventing goals scored against her, just as an impenetrable keeper can't build enough strength to score from her penalty box. So, this viewpoint extends to the individual and to the team. It's all part of the process.

A study was performed at Stanford University (David Paunesku, Gregory M. Walton, Carissa Romero, Eric N. Smith, David S. Yeager, and Carol S. Dweck) about the mindset that youth take on in stress with leads that are quite profound. In the study, researchers took a single child from a classroom and administered a fairly easy pen-and-paper test. When the researcher reported their score and commented on their performance, he used only one of two sentences: "You must be smart." or "You must have worked really hard."

Praised for either their intelligence or effort, they were then given a more difficult test. Their scores were naturally lower. Next, both groups were offered the chance to take yet another test. Ninety percent of those praised for their effort opted for the third test, and the majority of those praised for intelligence opted out, demoralized by their performance, as the study describes it.

This so eloquently describes the very core of one of my messages. Your daughter isn't a "winner," because that implies her trait is fixed. She found a way to win. There's a difference. "Winners" may have certain characteristics, but winners latch on to doing what it takes to win, not being entitled to it.

I think that winners know how to lose. They understand what losing means. They understand why losing matters. True winners don't stop at losses, so they see loss as the start, not the end. Success is fighting *through* losses to earn wins.

You see, I work with my "students" on winning as an attitude, not winning as a result, just as I do with myself. I have setbacks, flaws, and imperfection all over my "record of attempts," but this book serves as an example of that attitude's manifestation. I'm no perfect example, but I do think back to my sporting experience, launching my first, second, third, and fourth business. Is this a process? Or is it a trait? Of course it's a process! My traits a few years back would never allow me to grow from a small business owner to entrepreneur!

It also strikes me as important that this attitude allows us to do things we've never done before. Otherwise, we would be as we are, always and forever. We couldn't do the extraordinary or create something that we've never created before.

Suffering losses and failing is as important as winning, but winning isn't really about soccer, is it? If 99.9993% of all athletes do not play pro, what are we really preparing them for? What is it we get out of this?

It's no secret that many top CEOs were top athletes. But what about those who aren't top athletes? Does it become invalid to suggest that athletes who don't compete at top levels are still better employees, owners, workers, thinkers, and creatives? Being an athlete introduces you to things you surely encounter in life like loss, failure, pain, injury, creativity, self-regulation, and many other structures that are commonplace through the flow of life. However, given the nature of sport, athletes are introduced to these structures more frequently and earlier than in some other circumstances. When we realize that the growth that comes from the blends of losses and wins is truly the gem, we can embrace them, even appreciate them. As I say to my team each and every tough game, we win or we learn.

The point I'm making here is that we are here to support daughters in their approach to winning, not to label them as winners, losers, or otherwise and most certainly not to judge ourselves or her as a winner because of one performance.

My value as a coach is not determined by my record. Just like your value as a parent is not determined by the score of a game or championship.

A Win Is Never Enough

What's the four letter word we all want?

M-O-R-E.

Ever heard of a top athlete retiring after the biggest win of their career? (The only person I can think of is Michael Jordan, and what did he do? Oh, right. He couldn't stop. He came back.) There are no examples of this because we keep playing. We keep going. We don't stop with a win. We don't consider one win as being successful. We are successful when we can continue to win. That important distinction is why our perspective of winning is so deadly.

There are significant things that come from winning: accolades, dopamine, euphoria. Much more significance comes from losing. Losing is the crucible in which winners are truly formed, decorated by tears, pains, questions, fears, doubts, and the looming compulsion to walk away. I can show you ten champions who have endured more losses than wins. And even in their best moments, I bet they never forget their toughest losses. It's natural to fear loss, but there are major psychological complications. To defile what are already tough losses with badgering in the car or at home is just torture. Sports are great crucibles for forging better people. In so many aspects of life, especially today, we have accepted wrongs, full-fledged falsehoods, and placed value on simple, vacant lies. We better ourselves when we admit our flaws, debate our truths, and combat our weaknesses. And yet, I've seen fist fights after games. Referees have been assaulted after matches. And rival parent groups hurl insults across the half line. All because we aren't winning, might not win, or didn't win.

It's clear that these wins or losses were very personal to these parents. It was almost like they were playing. Or that they were being judged for this game's outcome. It mattered so much. I didn't get it. Even as a highly competitive person, the coach, and a man who wanted to watch my girls be victorious, I was uncomfortable by the weight of some games.

What have we got to prove from the sideline? It's not our game. It's not our battle.

At professional levels, or collegiate, or maybe even at a large national tournament, sure. I get it that tensions will run high. But that's for players. For us as leaders, I'm sure we could lead better, more effectively than what I've seen.

I once saw a coach stamp her feet, throw a clipboard, and scream across the field. It was a title game, but I still felt a lack of professionalism was present.

What was she so upset about?

Then after the game, I heard parents getting in arguments. A fight broke out. Meanwhile, during this catastrophe, I'm walking a player with a concussion to the trainer.

What really mattered here?

My Mom's Silence

In my senior year in high school in the northern part of Prince George's County, I was one of two white players on the team. I loved it. I joined with a high-level Latino soccer team, practicing in a school gym on weeknights. I was getting schooled week in and week out for 18 weeks before I earned my stripes. I was embarrassed daily—the comedy show for everyone else. I could take more punches than everyone else, though, and so I kept going back. One night, I reached for a ball, and while fully extended, caught an elbow to the upper thigh. I didn't play for the following six months—a torn quadriceps left me with little power and little likelihood to return to the game at all. I remember crying as I heard the doctors inform me that my soccer career was over. You've heard this story before.

Looking back, I see now that it was the catalyst for the shift in my psychological approach to problems. I was against insurmountable odds, but I defeated them. I never saw anything the same way again. Challenges are in everything we do. Life itself is a struggle for survival, and I now face challenges fearlessly. If I set my mind to it, I could win. I would beat the odds!

What was the win here? Was it making the team?

My mom, as much as she tried to tell me stark realities, always had my back. She was a true foundation. She let me do what I thought I needed to do to try. There was fire in me, just like there's fire in your daughter, but fire is hard to steer. I'm willing to bet Mom learned that the hard way, and eventually, she learned how best to support me, quietly, lovingly. She's a great example of what I wish I could offer to players. Love when they've lost, love when they've won.

No matter how much your daughter plays or loves to play, life isn't only about soccer, soccer isn't only about winning, and winning certainly doesn't stem only from soccer. That reminder comes in one form or another for coaches and parents of young athletes. Family events, school, and other realities set in, and we realize it's just a part of life, not all of it. Even for professional athletes, their craft is just one part of their world. They are people too. They have families, become mothers, build a life.

Earlier, we talked about the sheer numbers of youth sports, and how mathematically unlikely your player is to be the next Mia Hamm. Let that mathematical reminder come to you when you need it most—when you think this sport is everything to you and your team. It's not, and it shouldn't be.

There are over 400,000 youth soccer players. There are probably 45,000 games per weekend across all sports. Is your game that significant?

I'm sure you're very competitive. Competition has been a part of my life since I was four years old, and I don't expect that will change any time soon, but the field I play on now is much different than it was at age 10. I don't remember the wins that I experienced through most of my childhood soccer games. I remember some heart-breakers in high school and some paramount wins from those years, and I remember some college travel experiences, but not all of them. The truth is, we immortalize specific wins and losses for our daughters not because of their magnitude but because of our responses. It's as if the universe will collapse if we don't get that one win today! But here's the reality: The wins are great. The feelings of winning are great. Sharing them with your daughter, I'm sure, has no equivalent. But they are her wins to be shared with you. When we take the wins and losses too seriously, we distance ourselves from the real opportunity—the ability to connect on the value that a young woman owns whether they win or lose.

It's incredibly tough to be a young girl. I can't say I have experienced it, of course, but I can understand based on all the tears shed on my shoulder. What I do know is that if we, as the people they look up to, value them for their records, their wins, and their ability to produce a specific result at a certain time, we have lost them to the whims of the gig-economy's deepest trench where self-worth is measured just as much by real-life likes as it is on Instagram. Don't contribute to this evaluation method. Show up consistently through the wins and love your daughter.

Team Plight and the Orientation of Leadership

Let's say there are 10 teams locally. Let's say there are three levels of play: Elite, Premier, Challenger (top to bottom). They represent team skill level and performance. There are many clubs in your area, and you have options, but not every club has a team at each level, so an outline of your options might look like this:

	CLUB 1	CLUB 2	CLUB 3	CLUB 4
ELITE	A		F	H
PREMIER	B	D	G	I
CHALLENGER	C	E		J

If you look at the skill level, the Elite category has three teams: A, F and H. The Premier level has four. Note that in Club 2, there is no Elite level team.

Each year at tryouts, I have a flight of players leave team B with me to play on team D. While there is no level change, do you know how that team markets itself? "We're the top team in our age group! Be a part of the top team, and you'll be moving up!"

Have you been a part of this kind of team movement? Gotta love guerilla recruiting tactics for 13-year-olds. I get it. We want to build good teams and help our team level up. I see nothing wrong with that. But before you slam the door on this subject, let's make sure we understand why we're moving and who is making the choice. If she gets more playing time, I'm all for it. If she's going to be in a better environment, I'm all for it. But only if that's what she's asked for.

Some parents want the prestige of being on the "top" team. It's rooted in the ego, not love. It's just a side step, and what's not taken into account is who's coaching, the team environment, or any of the 990 other elements that you may find out when you make the switch. If you're someone who has been club-hopping to find the best fit, don't worry—hope is here.

This "grass is always greener" approach is broken for two fundamental reasons. First, you'll be doing more damage to your daughter's long-term play by switching teams more often than you can really account for with solid, rational reasons. It's like switching schools 18 times before you get your GED. There are very few kids who enjoy that. Second, you're asking a player to adapt to a new system over and over, rather than being able to develop a relationship that she trusts or a foundation.

Players certainly outgrow coaches, they want to test themselves, and they might not like the current team dynamic, but four hours of trying out isn't always enough to gauge what the player might be missing should she change teams. I've had more than 15 families leave my team, only to return later. I take pride in sharing that simply because I do believe that we coaches have relationships with players that can be sustainably empowering, but it takes some buy-in for the long run.

I've also had players leave only to detest a coach, hate the team, hate the game, and walk away.

Had a bad year? Welcome to a real job or relationship. Didn't get to play every minute of every game? Guess what, welcome to sports. Oh, you got invited to join another team midseason? Have the conversation about what it does to the team, to your daughter, and what it means to commit. The origin of the need to change teams is important. If it's you as a parent because you're not getting what you want or what you think your daughter wants or needs, you're being selfish. Enough young athletes play sports only to please their parents. No need to go above and beyond and force them to move teams and rewrite their entire psychological safety boundaries.

Sports is a long haul, and this isn't the WNBA. We're not making trades daily to build the best team. There are plenty of good reasons to switch; just make sure you're doing it because she wants to do it, not because you want to. Seek quality coaching, good leadership, and a sound soccer experience for your daughter before you favor team rankings, win percentage, or top-team-syndrome.

This is not a one-size-fits-all equation, but these might help if you're evaluating.

Good reasons to switch teams:

- Play with friends
- Coaching and leadership

- Level of play fits better with long term goals
- Team culture
- Club stance on development
- Play time

Reasons to question your motives to switch teams:

- Better team rank
- "Top" team in age (but maybe not a change in actual level of play)
- Uniform (you'd be surprised)
- Club prestige
- Cost (this is a reality, but is worth exploring because it's not about her)
- You want to win more

No matter what you do in selecting your team, remember that regardless of wins or losses, this isn't about you, and the record or status of the team is not a direct reflection of your value. We are the guides and supports for strong women to develop through sports, and no sideline behavior is less appropriate than ego-driven self-assessment and a manipulated sense of importance.

We are just observers to the real joy and growth of our young athletes.

Winning isn't about you. It's not for you.

It's all about her. Let her play, already!

CHAPTER 8

Habits for Life: Women Who Shape the World

"The most beautiful people we have known are those who have known defeat, known suffering, known struggle, known loss, and have found their way out of the depths. These persons have an appreciation, a sensitivity and an understanding of life that fills them with compassions, gentleness, and a deep loving concern. Beautiful people do not just happen."

– Elizabeth Kubler-Ross

The wonderful part about what we've been working on together over the last seven chapters is how it can all weave together to form a quilted foundation for young athletes to become their best. It's a wonderful thing when I see all of these things coalesce in an environment. It's so welcoming for the girls and so energizing as they caravan off into their successes. It really does make a difference.

I started this book because I feel that life is a great teacher, and sports a great lesson planner. When we step back and truly admire what can happen in sports, allow for healthy conversations, dialogue, and the release of ego, and couple it with support and honesty, what we can create is stunningly beautiful people—not physically, but mentally and emotionally.

I'd like to share with you two students of mine. Both have significant battles to overcome physically and both of the families have amazing relationships with their daughters. Relationships that have been forged through difficulty, a laissez-faire parental approach, and a level of love and respect for key elements of growth.

We'll call her Jen. Jen has an underdeveloped right arm from an injury at birth. Haven't heard her use it as an excuse yet, and I've worked with her for several years as she's outworked, outpaced, and out-earned her peers. She's now playing at the academy level, which, for all intents and purposes, means she's about as advanced as she can be for her age.

Then there's another student, we'll call her Joanne. She is allergic to everything. I mean everything. She's allergic to grass and can only eat 31 foods (more than 31 kinds of foods make up most single meals you and I consume regularly). She currently plays with a team that could very likely take a national championship this year or next.

Both of these athletes represent something I cherish deeply, but it's not what you'd expect. It's their parents. Their parents have worked to release their ego and needs and in doing so created amazing families that have allowed lessons to be learned, support to be offered, and as much interest as the kid has had to be fed. It's really a simple mechanism. It's being grounded.

Jen and Joanne represent something special. Yes, it's clear they must overcome the odds of a condition and find a way to get what they want, but the environment in which they are succeeding deserves the credit. It's easy for a young girl to be successful, no matter the odds, when we provide these essential things such as love, support, and non-judgement. We can't play the game for them, but we can provide the room for them. These two standout students are examples of products of something I value deeply: grounded parents who give them enough room to develop their craft and live their passion, without getting hung up on the rankings, the roster, and the minutes. When I get the chance to meet families that "get it," it's usually plain to see. The parents are pleasant to talk to, ask about other elements of my world, ask for insights on how to best support their daughter, and share things that help me understand the whole person that she is becoming.

Most importantly though, the "success" that I see in

them is not their athletic success. They are top level players because they love the game and intentionally decided to pursue it. But there are hundreds of other examples of families like this who have players in recreational leagues or who decided they love something more than their first sport-love. Both are okay, because what these families really represent is success in family dialogue, open conversations, and how their girls see the world.

Those girls understand hard work, they get what it takes to achieve, and they will be successful at their soccer career just like their relationships and college and whatever else they pursue. They have good habits. They have a good mindset. And their parents supported the process over the product.

When we allow our young athletes to develop a process that leads to success, we empower them to shape a belief in themselves.

As you turn these last few pages, bear in mind in terms of my stories that the extremes are illustrated intentionally so I can craft my argument, but sometimes the subtlety of our language and the off-the-field, casual interactions with young women is where the damage is done.

As we close in on the real meaning behind all of this, let's be sure we understand that the excuses we give to our girls are the ones that shackle them to the floor. Let's give them rocket fuel instead.

Our Habit Becomes Her Normal

"The difference between a broken community and a thriving one is the presence of women who are valued."
Michelle Obama

Young people pick up on so much more than we realize. I've been around my friends' really young kids and found it so fascinating how much, especially given my healthy distance, they repeat and resemble their parents in action. Mannerisms, ways of speaking, body language are all picked up through the eyes of a child.

This presents a wonderful opportunity to recognize our own habits, because they will become the imprints on our players. I've noticed this even with older teams. They model the same kind of behaviors I do. That may only be while with me, or on the field, or in the way they handle games and challenges on the field, but it's real that they mimic what they see and look up to.

You're a strong source of tremendous influence. Even teenage girls, who may not seem like they ever could, are picking up on adult behaviors to define the way they see the world. They still need role models, examples of quality, and support.

Bearing the burden of reconciling our past requires us to look inward and bring our best to these young women to offer them a boundless plain of opportunity at their feet, even if that means we must struggle to paint that plain for them. What I'm asking you to do is nothing short of ultra-challenging. I'm asking you to look past your own moments, wants, needs, ego, and habits to see how your behaviors might be influencing your daughter. It's a tall order.

And yet, here I am, making the ask. You and I have something in common. We want your daughter to be the best she can be. Don't we want her to be a leader? To act out of integrity? To live her life fully, so as to experience the full range of the human experience?

Of course, we do. So our goal is to create a belief that enables that, and in doing so, we have to understand what the real objective is as leaders. As we interact with our future women leaders on a regular basis, keep these in mind as end goals for any future woman in leadership:

- *High self-worth that's not determined outwardly but inwardly*
- *Independence and interdependence among teams*
- *Comfort with failure and risk-taking*
- *Ability to lead and be led*
- *Emotional intelligence to handle loss, failure, and mistakes*
- *Experience being creative to know when to follow an example and when to set one*
- *Routines of practicing that yield results*
- *The ability to prioritize the long term returns despite short term setbacks*

As we caregivers continue to craft the environment in which an awesome wave of future female leaders will grow, it's imperative we self-assess for our youth will surely mimic what they see. To raise the best leaders, mothers, friends, and daughters, we have to continuously assess whether they are getting what they need.

There's a lot of gray area in the concept of "what they need," but I believe that we have the ability as parents, coaches, mentors, and friends to walk that gray area with great and noble intention. Sometimes that means letting someone fail, so that they can learn to stand themselves up again. Watch a really young child fall and notice how they look up before they actually react. Play it cool, and they'll get up and on their way. Panic, and all hell breaks loose. A small bit of positive encouragement can do wonders for a young player. Much of the way our kids handle stress and failure is a reflection of the way we've taught them to.

The youth sport experience, in my humblest of opinions, is the most meaningful way to allow young leaders to see what they could become. It's a means by which we craft powerful women who understand things that happen in the real world.

They aren't afraid of being measured. They understand failure. They understand what "working when no one is looking" stands to help them create. They fight despite the odds.

If we are consistently driving our daughter's sports experience as a means to satisfy our ego, unfinished business, or incomplete dreams, we are robbing her of her own opportunities and stifling her growth.

So what are your habits in the sport and what examples are you giving her for leadership?

If you show up for her, she'll show up for herself when it matters, because she'll know what it means to show up. So, use this time to think about which ways you're showing up for her and giving her an example of what's possible for her future.

- What language do you use?
- What kind of dialogue and conversation do you foster?
- What kind of safety do you create?
- What kind of values are made clear?
- What actions do you take that put her first?
- What supports do you offer her that make it clear that this isn't about you?

Your habits are your influence on others, your kids especially. Mind your habits.

The One Liners

I once had a coach in high school who said over and over, "Your stock is rising." whenever a player was showing improvement. I like this concept, more now than at any point in the past. When we learn to be a part of a bigger picture, we learn to place value upon ourselves and our contribution. For young women, this can be challenging, but certainly an important part of their development, so remember that it's your perspective that allows her to value herself and to trust herself to handle life.

If you think back to the preface, you'll recall two stories. One of a coach belittling a girl. One of a coach believing in a girl.

We've all, at some point in our life, had someone tell us we were nothing. That moment, wherever yours was, may have shaped you forever.

Soon, you won't be able to call the coach with issues or a complaint, because the coach will be her boss. Soon, you won't be able to yell at her in the car, because she'll have her own. Soon, you will be able to recount all the great memories, because you'll be growing and changing in the most magnificent of ways so that she may become her best self.

And all the while, you'll be the awakened parent on the sideline, so that when someone is yelling fervently at their daughter on the court or pitch or field, or screaming at a referee about a missed call, or shaking a fist at the coach for pulling his or her daughter out of the game, you can smile, take a deep breath, and whisper to yourself, *Let Her Play.*

Thank you,
AV

About the Author

Aaron has coached youth soccer on the girl's side of renowned Baltimore soccer club, Pipeline Soccer Club, for nearly a decade after NCAA Division I play. His experiences, the good, bad, and ugly, are shared in light of deep conversations and emotional understanding of what female athletes need most to be successful on and off the field.

Aaron wears the leadership hat in many forms. He's the CEO of an impact company called Ortus Academy, developing financial education technology and programs for Gen Z and Millennials. He's an active artist, business coach, and leads a community of heart-led entrepreneurs, giving this book a breadth of leadership and culture creation for your family, no matter what sport your daughter plays.

His work encompasses education, writing, and travels and expeditions around the globe. You can learn more about him on his website **www.aaronvelky.com** or you can visit his Instagram at @aaronvelky.

You are also welcome to join the dialogue about your daughter and her sport experience in the *Let Her Play Community* on Facebook!

Made in the USA
Middletown, DE
28 March 2020

87306794R00096